W 575 BRI

ABC OF SMOKING CESSATION

ABC OF SMOKING CESSATION

Edited by

JOHN BRITTON

Professor of Epidemiology at the University of Nottingham

First published 2004

ISBN 0 7279 1818 4

A catalogue record for this title is available from the British Library and the Library of Congress

The cover shows a No Smoking sign. With permission from Dennis Potokar/Science Photo Library

Set by BMJ Electronic Production
Printed and bound in Spain by GraphyCems, Navarra

Commissioning Editor: Eleanor Lines
Development Editor: Sally Carter/Nick Morgan
Production Controller: Mirjana Misina

For further information on Blackwell Publishing, visit our website:
http://www.blackwellpublishing.com

The publisher's policy is to use permanent paper from mills that operate a sustainable forestry policy, and
which has been manufactured from pulp processed using acid-free and elementary chlorine-free practices.
Furthermore, the publisher ensures that the text paper and cover board used have met acceptable
environmental accreditation standards.

Contents

Contributors

John Britton
Professor of Epidemiology at the University of Nottingham in the division of epidemiology and public health at City Hospital, Nottingham

Tim Coleman
Senior Lecturer in general practice at the School of Community Health Sciences in the Division of Primary Care at University Hospital, Queen's Medical Centre, Nottingham

Richard Edwards
Senior Lecturer in public health in the Evidence for Population Health Unit at the Medical School, University of Manchester

Christine Godfrey
Professor of Health Economics at the Department of Health Sciences and Centre for Health Economics at the University of York

Konrad Jamrozik
Professor of Primary Care Epidemiology, Imperial College, London, and Visiting Professor in Public Health, School of Population Health, University of Western Australia, Perth

Martin J Jarvis
Professor of Health Psychology in the Cancer Research UK Health Behaviour Unit, Department of Epidemiology and Public Health at the University College London

Ann McNeill
Independent consultant in public health and Honorary Senior Lecturer in the Psychology Department at St George's Hospital Medical School, London

Andrew Molyneux
Consultant respiratory physician at the Sherwood Forest Hospitals Trust, Nottinghamshire

Steve Parrott
Research Fellow at the Centre for Health Economics at the University of York

Elin Roddy
Clinical Research Fellow at the University of Nottingham in the Division of Respiratory Medicine at City Hospital, Nottingham

Penny Spice
Head of Public Involvement at Rushcliffe Primary Care Trust and formerly smoking cessation coordinator at Nottingham Health Authority

Robert West
Professor of Health Psychology in the Cancer Research UK Health Behaviour Unit, Department of Epidemiology and Public Health at the University College London

Preface

Smoking kills more people than any other avoidable factor in developed countries. Smoking cessation has a substantial positive impact on quantity and quality of life expectancy in all smokers, and smoking cessation interventions are among the most cost effective interventions available in medicine. It is therefore surprising that in many countries, smoking cessation measures are not routinely available or are not widely used to help smokers to quit smoking. Most medical schools do not train doctors properly to treat smoking, and many doctors and other health professionals are still unfamiliar with the basic underlying principles of smoking as an addictive behaviour, and with methods of intervening to help smokers to quit.

This book is intended to provide the basic, simple information needed to equip all health professionals to intervene effectively, efficiently, and constructively to help their patients to stop smoking. The book describes how and why people start smoking, why they continue to smoke, and what to do to help them to stop. We describe methods of ensuring that identifying and treating smoking becomes a routine component of health care, and because the best results are generally achieved by specialist smoking cessation services we describe some of the challenges and difficulties of establishing these facilities. As prevention of smoking in populations is such an important determinant of individual motivation to quit or avoid smoking, the authors summarise the population strategies and political policies that can help drive down the prevalence of smoking. For our managers, this ABC covers the cost-effectiveness of these initiatives.

One of the tragedies of modern clinical medicine is that treating smoking is so simple, has so much to offer, and so often is not done. The methods are not difficult. This book explains them.

John Britton

1 The problem of tobacco smoking

Richard Edwards

Cigarette smoking is the single biggest avoidable cause of death and disability in developed countries. Smoking is now increasing rapidly throughout the developing world and is one of the biggest threats to current and future world health. For most smokers, quitting smoking is the single most important thing they can do to improve their health. Encouraging smoking cessation is one of the most effective and cost effective things that doctors and other health professionals can do to improve health and prolong their patients' lives. This book will explore the reasons why smokers smoke, how to help them to quit, and how to reduce the prevalence of smoking more generally.

Who smokes tobacco?

Cigarette smoking first became a mass phenomenon in the United Kingdom and other more affluent countries in the early 20th century after the introduction of cheap, mass produced, manufactured cigarettes. Typically, a "smoking epidemic" in a population develops in four stages: a rise and then decline in smoking prevalence, followed two to three decades later by a similar trend in smoking related diseases. Usually, the uptake and consequent adverse effects of smoking occur earlier and to a greater degree among men.

In the United Kingdom there are about 13 million smokers, and worldwide an estimated 1.2 billion. Half of these smokers will die prematurely of a disease caused by their smoking, losing an average of eight years of life; this currently represents four million smokers each year worldwide. Deaths from smoking are projected to increase to more than 10 million a year by 2030, by which time 70% of deaths will be in developing countries.

The prevalence of smoking among adults in the United Kingdom has declined steadily from peaks in the 1940s in men and the late 1960s in women. However, this reduction in overall prevalence during stage 4 of the epidemic disguises relatively static levels of smoking among socioeconomically disadvantaged groups, making smoking one of the most important determinants of social inequalities in health in the developed world. Smoking has also declined much more slowly among young adults in the United Kingdom. The decline in smoking in the United Kingdom and some other developed countries may now be coming to an end. For example, since 1994 the prevalence of smoking in UK adults has remained at about 28%.

Whereas countries in western Europe, Australasia, and the United States may be in stage 4 of the smoking epidemic, in many developing countries the epidemic is just beginning. Smoking in low and middle income countries is increasing rapidly—for example, the prevalence of smoking among males in populous Asian countries is now far higher than in Western countries—45% in India, 53% in Japan, 63% in China, 69% in Indonesia, and 73% in Vietnam.

Adverse health effects

The adverse health effects of smoking are extensive, and have been exhaustively documented. There is a strong dose-response

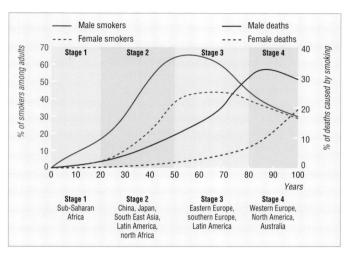

Stages of worldwide tobacco epidemic. Adapted from Lopez et al. A descriptive model of the cigarette epidemic in developed countries. *Tobacco Control* 1994;3:242-7

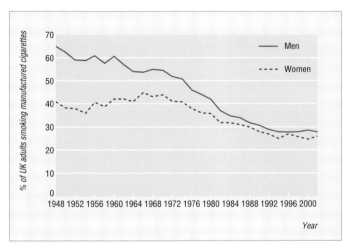

Prevalence of smoking of manufactured cigarettes in Great Britain. Data from Tobacco Advisory Council (1948-70) and general household survey (1972-2001)

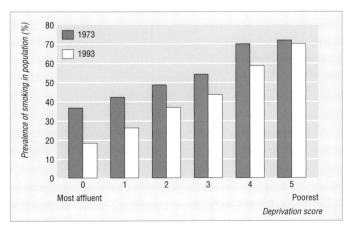

Cigarette smoking by deprivation level in Great Britain. Data from general household survey

relation with heavy smoking, duration of smoking, and early uptake associated with higher risks of smoking related disease and mortality. Data from 40 years of follow up of smokers in a prospective cohort study of male British doctors show the impact of smoking on longevity at different levels of exposure. The strongest cause-specific associations are with respiratory cancers and chronic obstructive pulmonary disease; in numeric terms, the greatest health impacts of smoking are on respiratory and cardiovascular diseases.

Some of the increases in health risk associated with smoking are greater among younger smokers. The risk of heart attack among smokers, for example, is at least double over the age of 60 years, but those aged under 50 have a more than fivefold increase in risk. Smokers are also at greater risk of many other non-fatal diseases, including osteoporosis, periodontal disease, impotence, male infertility, and cataracts. Smoking in pregnancy is associated with increased rates of fetal and perinatal death and reduced birth weight for gestational age. Passive smoking after birth is associated with cot death and respiratory disease in childhood and lung cancer, heart disease, and stroke in adults.

The effect on health services is considerable—for example, an estimated 364 000 admissions and £1.5bn ($2.4bn; €2.1bn) a year in health service costs are attributable to smoking in the United Kingdom alone.

Health benefits of smoking cessation

Stopping smoking has substantial immediate and long term health benefits for smokers of all ages. The excess risk of death from smoking falls soon after cessation and continues to do so for at least 10-15 years. Former smokers live longer than continuing smokers, no matter what age they stop smoking, though the impact of quitting on mortality is greatest at younger ages. For smokers who stop before age 35, survival is about the same as that for non-smokers.

The rate and extent of reduction of risk varies between diseases—for lung cancer the risk falls over 10 years to about 30%-50% that of continuing smokers, but the risk remains raised even after 20 years of abstinence. There is benefit from quitting at all ages, but stopping before age 30 removes 90% of the lifelong risk of lung cancer. The excess risk of oral and oesophageal cancer caused by smoking is halved within five years of cessation.

The risk of heart disease decreases much more quickly after quitting smoking. Within a year the excess mortality due to smoking is halved, and within 15 years the absolute risk is almost the same as in people who have never smoked. In a meta-analysis by Wilson and colleagues in 2000, the odds ratio for death for smokers who stopped smoking after myocardial infarction was 0.54, a far higher protective effect than the 0.75-0.88 odds ratio for death achieved by the conventional standard treatments for myocardial infarction, including thrombolysis, aspirin, β blockers, and statins. Smoking cessation also reduces the risk of death after a stroke and of death from pneumonia and influenza.

Smoking is associated with an accelerated rate of decline in lung function with age. Cessation results in a small increase in lung function and reverses the effect on subsequent rate of decline, which reverts to that in non-smokers.

Thus, early cessation is especially important in susceptible individuals to prevent or delay the onset of chronic obstructive pulmonary disease. In patients with this disease, mortality and symptoms are reduced in former smokers compared with continuing smokers. Recent evidence shows that the benefits

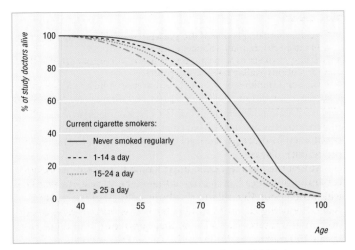

Survival by smoking status, according to study of male British doctors (follow up after 40 years, 1951-91). Adapted from Doll et al (see Further Reading box)

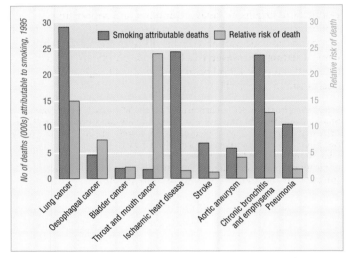

Numbers and relative risk of death (by cause) due to smoking, United Kingdom. Data from Tobacco Advisory Group of the Royal College of Physicians and Doll et al (see Further Reading box)

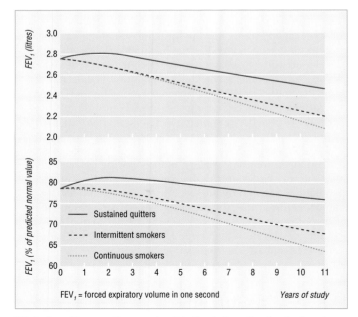

Effect of smoking cessation on rate of decline in lung function in chronic obstructive pulmonary disease. Adapted from Anthonisen et al. *Am J Respir Crit Care Med* 2002;166:675-9

Key points

- Cigarette smoking is one of the greatest avoidable causes of premature death and disability in the world
- Helping smokers to stop smoking is one of the most cost effective interventions available in clinical practice
- Promoting smoking cessation should therefore be a major priority in all countries and for all health professionals in all clinical settings

Stopping smoking before or in the first three to four months of pregnancy protects the fetus against the reduced birth weight associated with smoking. Preoperative cessation reduces perioperative mortality and complications

occur even in older patients with severe chronic obstructive pulmonary disease.

At a population level, the importance of smoking cessation is paramount. Peto has estimated that current cigarette smoking will cause about 450 million deaths worldwide in the next 50 years. Reducing current smoking by 50% would prevent 20-30 million premature deaths in the first quarter of this century and about 150 million in the second quarter. Preventing young people from starting smoking would have a more delayed but ultimately even greater impact on mortality.

Effective prevention of cigarette smoking and help for those wishing to quit can therefore yield enormous health benefits for populations and individuals. Promoting and supporting smoking cessation should be an important health policy priority in all countries and for healthcare professionals in all clinical settings. However, this has not so far generally been reflected at a policy level or in the practice of individual healthcare professionals.

Competing interests: RE is chairman of North West ASH (Action on Smoking and Health); he receives no financial reward for this work. JB has been reimbursed by GlaxoWellcome (now GlaxoSmithKline) for attending two international conferences, has received a speaker's honorarium from GlaxoWellcome, and has been the principal investigator in a clinical trial of nicotine replacement therapy funded by Pharmacia. Both these companies manufacture nicotine replacement products.

Further reading

- Tobacco Advisory Group of the Royal College of Physicians. *Nicotine addiction in Britain*. London: Royal College of Physicians of London, 2000. www.rcplondon.ac.uk/pubs/books/nicotine/index.htm
- Jha P, Chaloupka F, eds. *Tobacco control in developing countries*. Oxford: Oxford University Press, 1999.
- Doll R, Peto R, Wheatley K, Gray R, Sutherland I. Mortality in relation to smoking: 40 years' observations on male British doctors. *BMJ* 1994;309:901-11.
- World Bank. *Curbing the epidemic: governments and the economics of tobacco control*. Washington, DC: World Bank, 1999. www1.worldbank.org/tobacco/reports.asp
- US Department of Health and Human Services. *The health benefits of smoking cessation: a report of the surgeon general*. Rockville, MD: US Government Printing Office, 1990. (DHHS publication No (CDC) 90-8416.)
- Wilson K, Willan A, Cook D. Effect of smoking cessation on mortality after myocardial infarction. *Arch Intern Med* 2000;160:939-44.

2 Why people smoke

Martin J Jarvis

For much of the 20th century, smoking was regarded as a socially learned habit and as a personal choice. It is only in the past decade or so that the fundamental role of nicotine in sustaining smoking behaviour has begun to be more widely accepted. It is now recognised that cigarette smoking is primarily a manifestation of nicotine addiction and that smokers have individually characteristic preferences for their level of nicotine intake. Smokers regulate the way they puff and inhale to achieve their desired nicotine dose.

The link with nicotine addiction does not imply that pharmacological factors drive smoking behaviour in a simple way and to the exclusion of other influences. Social, economic, personal, and political influences all play an important part in determining patterns of smoking prevalence and cessation. Although drug effects underpin the behaviour, family and wider social influences are often critical in determining who starts smoking, who gives up, and who continues.

Why do people start smoking?

Experimenting with smoking usually occurs in the early teenage years and is driven predominantly by psychosocial motives. For a beginner, smoking a cigarette is a symbolic act conveying messages such as, in the words of the tobacco company Philip Morris, "I am no longer my mother's child," and "I am tough." Children who are attracted to this adolescent assertion of perceived adulthood or rebelliousness tend to come from backgrounds that favour smoking (for example, with high levels of smoking in parents, siblings, and peers; relatively deprived neighbourhoods; schools where smoking is common). They also tend not to be succeeding according to their own or society's terms (for example, they have low self esteem, have impaired psychological wellbeing, are overweight, or are poor achievers at school).

The desired image is sufficient for the novice smoker to tolerate the aversion of the first few cigarettes, after which pharmacological factors assume much greater importance. Again in the words of Philip Morris, "as the force from the psychosocial symbolism subsides, the pharmacological effect takes over to sustain the habit." Within a year or so of starting to smoke, children inhale the same amount of nicotine per cigarette as adults, experience craving for cigarettes when they cannot smoke, make attempts to quit, and report experiencing the whole range of nicotine withdrawal symptoms.

Physical and psychological effects of nicotine

Absorption of cigarette smoke from the lung is rapid and complete, producing with each inhalation a high concentration arterial bolus of nicotine that reaches the brain within 10-16 seconds, faster than by intravenous injection. Nicotine has a distributional half life of 15-20 minutes and a terminal half life in blood of two hours. Smokers therefore experience a pattern of repetitive and transient high blood nicotine concentrations from each cigarette, with regular hourly cigarettes needed to maintain raised concentrations, and overnight blood levels dropping to close to those of non-smokers.

"If it were not for the nicotine in tobacco smoke, people would be little more inclined to smoke than they are to blow bubbles"

M A H Russell, tobacco researcher, 1974

Smoking a cigarette for a beginner is a symbolic act of rebellion

By age 20, 80% of cigarette smokers regret that they ever started, but as a result of their addiction to nicotine, many will continue to smoke for a substantial proportion of their adult lives

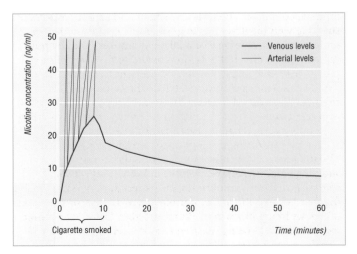

Arterial and venous levels of nicotine during cigarette smoking

Nicotine has pervasive effects on brain neurochemistry. It activates nicotinic acetylcholine receptors (nAChRs), which are widely distributed in the brain, and induces the release of dopamine in the nucleus accumbens. This effect is the same as that produced by other drugs of misuse (such as amphetamines and cocaine) and is thought to be a critical feature of brain addiction mechanisms. Nicotine is a psychomotor stimulant, and in new users it speeds simple reaction time and improves performance on tasks of sustained attention. However, tolerance to many of these effects soon develops, and chronic users probably do not continue to obtain absolute improvements in performance, cognitive processing, or mood. Smokers typically report that cigarettes calm them down when they are stressed and help them to concentrate and work more effectively, but little evidence exists that nicotine provides effective self medication for adverse mood states or for coping with stress.

A plausible explanation for why smokers perceive cigarettes to be calming may come from a consideration of the effects of nicotine withdrawal. Smokers start to experience impairment of mood and performance within hours of their last cigarette, and certainly overnight. These effects are completely alleviated by smoking a cigarette. Smokers go through this process thousands of times over the course of their smoking career, and this may lead them to identify cigarettes as effective self medication, even if the effect is the negative one of withdrawal relief rather than any absolute improvement.

Symptoms of nicotine withdrawal

Much of the intractability of cigarette smoking is thought to stem from the problems of withdrawal symptoms—particularly irritability, restlessness, feeling miserable, impaired concentration, and increased appetite—as well as from cravings for cigarettes. These withdrawal symptoms begin within hours of the last cigarette and are at maximal intensity for the first week. Most of the affective symptoms then resolve over three or four weeks, but hunger can persist for several months. Cravings, sometimes intense, can also persist for many months, especially if triggered by situational cues.

Social and behavioural aspects

The primary reinforcing properties of nicotine ultimately sustain smoking behaviour: in experimental models, if nicotine is removed from cigarette smoke, or nicotine's effects on the central nervous system are blocked pharmacologically, smoking eventually ceases. However, under normal conditions, the intimate coupling of behavioural rituals and sensory aspects of smoking with nicotine uptake gives ample opportunities for secondary conditioning. For a 20 a day smoker, "puff by puff" delivery of nicotine to the brain is linked to the sight of the packet, the smell of the smoke, and the scratch in the throat some 70 000 times each year. This no doubt accounts for smokers' widespread concern that if they stopped smoking they would not know what to do with their hands, and for the ability of smoking related cues to evoke strong cravings.

Social influences also operate to modulate nicotine's effects. The direction of this influence can be to discourage smoking—as, for example, with the cultural disapproval of smoking in some communities, the expectation of non-smoking that has become the norm in professional groups, or the effects of smoke-free policies in workplaces. Other factors encourage smoking, such as being married to a smoker or being part of social networks in socially disadvantaged groups, among whom prevalence is so high as to constitute a norm.

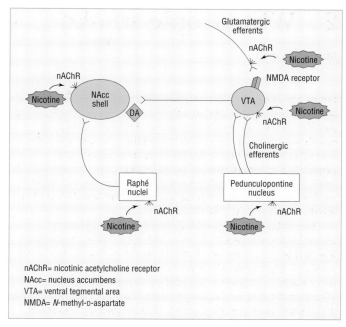

nAChR= nicotinic acetylcholine receptor
NAcc= nucleus accumbens
VTA= ventral tegmental area
NMDA= N-methyl-D-aspartate

Pathways of nicotine reinforcement and addiction. Adapted from Watkins et al. *Nicotine and Tobacco Research* 2000;2:19-37

Effects of nicotine withdrawal

Symptom	Duration	Incidence (%)
Lightheadedness	<48 hours	10
Sleep disturbance	<1 week	25
Poor concentration	<2 weeks	60
Craving for nicotine	<2 weeks	70
Irritability or aggression	<4 weeks	50
Depression	<4 weeks	60
Restlessness	<4 weeks	60
Increased appetite	<10 weeks	70

Many experimental and clinical studies have shown that withdrawal symptoms are attributable to nicotine, as nicotine replacement (by gum, patch, spray, or lozenge) reliably attenuates the severity of withdrawal

Behavioural rituals are closely coupled with sensory aspects of smoking

Regulation of nicotine intake

Smokers show a strong tendency to regulate their nicotine intakes from cigarettes within quite narrow limits. They avoid intakes that are either too low (provoking withdrawal) or too high (leading to unpleasant effects of nicotine overdose). Within individuals, nicotine preferences emerge early in the smoking career and seem to be stable over time. The phenomenon of nicotine titration is responsible for the failure of intakes to decline after switching to cigarettes with low tar and nicotine yields. Compensatory puffing and inhalation, operating at a subconscious level, ensure that nicotine intakes are maintained. As nicotine and tar delivery in smoke are closely coupled, compensatory smoking likewise maintains tar intake and defeats any potential health gain from lower tar cigarettes. Similar compensatory behaviour occurs after cutting down on the number of cigarettes smoked each day; hence this popular strategy fails to deliver any meaningful health benefits.

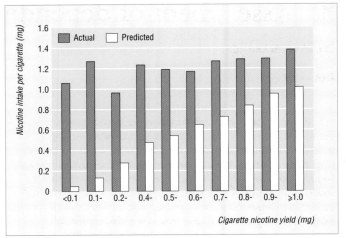

Regulation of nicotine intake: actual and predicted intake per cigarette from low tar cigarettes. Data from health survey for England, 1998

Socioeconomic status and nicotine addiction

An emerging phenomenon of the utmost significance over the past two decades has been the increasing association of continued smoking with markers of social disadvantage. Among affluent men and women in the United Kingdom, the proportion of ever smokers who have quit has more than doubled since the early 1970s, from about 25% to nearly 60%, whereas in the poorest groups the proportion has remained at around 10%. Part of the explanation for this phenomenon may be found in the growing evidence that poorer smokers tend to have higher levels of nicotine intake and are substantially more dependent on nicotine. It is evident that future progress in reducing smoking is increasingly going to have to tackle the problems posed by poverty.

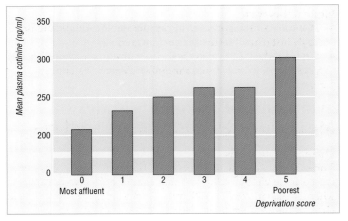

Nicotine intake and social deprivation. Data from health survey for England (1993, 1994, 1996)

Smoking as a chronic disease

Cigarette dependence is a chronic relapsing condition that for many users entails a struggle to achieve long term abstinence that extends over years or decades. Successful interventions need to tackle the interacting constellation of factors—personal, family, socioeconomic, and pharmacological—that sustain use and can act as major barriers to cessation.

Further reading

- Royal College of Physicians. *Nicotine addiction in Britain*. London: RCP, 2000.
- Benowitz NL. Pharmacologic aspects of cigarette smoking and nicotine addiction. *N Engl J Med* 1988;319:1318-30.
- National Institutes of Health. *Risks associated with smoking cigarettes with low machine-measured yields of tar and nicotine*. Bethesda, MD: Department of Health and Human Services, National Institutes of Health, National Cancer Institute, 2001. (NIH publication No 02-5074.)
- Jarvis MJ. Patterns and predictors of unaided smoking cessation in the general population. In: Bolliger CT, Fagerstrom KO, eds. *The tobacco epidemic*. Basle: Karger, 1997:151-64.

The photo of children smoking is with permission from Ralph Mortimer/Rex, and the photo of the man smoking is with permission from Alexandra Murphy/Photonica.

Competing interests: MJJ has received speaker's honorariums from GlaxoSmithKline and Pharmacia. He is also director of an NHS funded smoking cessation clinic. See chapter 1 for the series editor's competing interests.

Smoking behaviour and cessation

- The natural course of cigarette smoking is typically characterised by the onset of regular smoking in adolescence, followed by repeated attempts to quit
- Each year about a third of adult smokers in the United Kingdom try to quit, usually unaided and typically relapsing within days
- In general, less than 3% of attempts to quit result in sustained (12 months') cessation, though the chances of success are slightly higher in women of childbearing age, parents of young children, and spouses of non-smokers

Key points

- Smoking usually starts as a symbolic act of rebellion or maturity
- By age 20, 80% of smokers regret having started to smoke
- Nicotine from cigarettes is highly addictive—probably because it is delivered so rapidly to the brain
- Smoking a cigarette, especially the first of the day, feels good mainly because it reverses the symptoms of nicotine withdrawal
- Most smokers who switch to low tar cigarettes or reduce the number of cigarettes they smoke continue to inhale the same amount of nicotine, and hence tar, from the cigarettes they smoke
- Heavy dependence on nicotine is strongly related to socioeconomic disadvantage
- Smoking is a chronic relapsing addictive disease

3 Assessment of dependence and motivation to stop smoking

Robert West

Whether a smoker succeeds in stopping smoking depends on the balance between that individual's motivation to stop smoking and his or her degree of dependence on cigarettes. Clinicians must be able to assess both of these characteristics. Motivation is important because "treatments" to assist with smoking cessation will not work in smokers who are not highly motivated. Dependence is especially important in smokers who do want to stop smoking, as it influences the choice of intervention. It is also important to bear in mind that:
● Motivation to stop and dependence are often related to each other: heavy smokers may show low motivation because they lack confidence in their ability to quit; lighter smokers may show low motivation because they believe they can stop in the future if they wish
● Motivation to stop can vary considerably with time and be strongly influenced by the immediate environment
● What smokers say about their wish to stop, especially in a clinical interview, may not accurately reflect their genuine feelings.

Measuring dependence in smokers

Qualitative methods
The simplest approach to measuring dependence on cigarettes is a basic qualitative approach that uses questions to find out whether the smoker has difficulty in refraining from smoking in circumstances when he or she would normally smoke or whether the smoker has made a serious attempt to stop in the past but failed.

Quantitative methods
The most commonly used quantitative measure of dependence is the Fagerstrom test for nicotine dependence, which has proved successful in predicting the outcome of attempts to stop. The higher the score on this questionnaire, the higher the level of dependence: smokers in the general population score an average of about 4 on this scale. Of all the items in the questionnaire, cigarettes per day and time to first cigarette of the day seem to be the most important indicators of dependence.

Objective methods
The concentration of nicotine or its metabolite, cotinine, in blood, urine, or saliva is often used in research as an objective index of dependence because it provides an accurate measure of the quantity of nicotine consumed, which is itself a marker of dependence. Carbon monoxide concentration of expired air is a measure of smoke intake over preceding hours; it is not as accurate an intake measure as nicotine based measures, but it is much less expensive and gives immediate feedback to the smoker.

How should dependence influence choice of treatment?
The main value of measuring dependence in tailoring cessation interventions to individual smokers is in the choice of pharmacotherapy. The manufacturers of smoking cessation drug products (principally nicotine replacement therapy and bupropion—see later chapters in this book) recommend that

This article reviews some simple methods to assess dependence and motivation in smokers

Dependence	Motivation	
	Low	High
Low	● Unlikely to stop but could do so without help ● Primary intervention goal is to increase motivation	● Likely to stop with minimal help ● Primary intervention goal is to trigger a quit attempt
High	● Unlikely to stop ● Primary intervention goal is initially to increase motivation to make smoker receptive to treatment for dependence	● Unlikely to stop without help but would benefit from treatment ● Primary intervention goal is to engage smoker in treatment

Clinical intervention goals for smoking according to dependence and motivation to quit

Do you find it difficult not to smoke in situations where you would normally do so?	No/Yes
Have you tried to stop smoking for good in the past but found that you could not?	No/Yes

A "yes" response to either of these questions would suggest that the smoker might benefit from help with stopping

Q1. How many cigarettes per day do you usually smoke? (Write a number in the box and circle one response)	10 or less	0
	11 to 20	1
	21 to 30	2
	31 or more	3
Q2. How soon after you wake up do you smoke your first cigarette? (Circle one response)	Within 5 minutes	3
	6-30 minutes	2
	31 or more	0
Q3. Do you find it difficult to stop smoking in non-smoking areas? (Circle one response)	No	0
	Yes	1
Q4. Which cigarette would you most hate to give up? (Circle one response)	First of the morning	1
	Other	0
Q5. Do you smoke more frequently in the first hours after waking than the rest of the day? (Circle one response)	No	0
	Yes	1
Q4. Do you smoke if you are so ill that you are in bed most of the day? (Circle one response)	No	0
	Yes	1

The Fagerstrom test for nicotine dependence: a quantitative index of dependence. The numbers in the pink shaded column corresponding to the smoker's responses are added together to produce a single score on scale of 0 (low dependence) to 10 (high dependence). Adapted from Heatherton et al. *Br J Addict* 1991;86:1119-27

only smokers of 10 or more cigarettes a day should use their products. However, the UK National Institute for Clinical Excellence has recently recognised this cut off to be arbitrary and has not specified any particular lower limit for daily cigarette consumption.

Measuring motivation to stop smoking

Survey evidence in the United Kingdom shows that about two thirds of smokers declare that they want to stop smoking and that in any year almost a third make an attempt to stop. Young smokers are widely believed to be less motivated to stop than older smokers, but in fact the reverse is true: older smokers are typically less motivated.

However, only a minority of smokers attempting to stop currently use smoking cessation medications or attend a specialist cessation service. This may reflect a lack of confidence among smokers that these treatments will help.

Direct questioning
Motivation to stop can be assessed qualitatively by means of simple direct questions about their interest and intentions to quit. This simple approach is probably sufficient for most clinical practice, although slightly more complex, semiquantitative measures (asking the smoker to rate degree of desire to stop on a scale from "not at all" to "very much") can also be used.

Stages of change
One model of the process of behaviour change has become popular: the "transtheoretical model." In this model, smokers are assigned to one of five stages of motivation: precontemplation (not wishing to stop), contemplation (thinking about stopping but not in the near future), preparation (planning to stop in the near future), action (trying to stop), and maintenance (have stopped for some time). Smokers may cycle through the contemplation to action stages many times before stopping for good. This model has been widely adopted, though no evidence exists that the rather elaborate questionnaires for assigning smokers to particular stages predict smoking cessation better than the simple direct questions outlined above.

Some clinicians use a smoker's degree of motivation to stop as a prognostic indicator of likely success once the quit attempt has been decided. In fact, degree of motivation seems to play a fairly small role in success; once a quit attempt is made, markers of dependence are far stronger determinants of success. The ultimate practical objective of assessing motivation is therefore to identify smokers who are ready to make a quit attempt. After that, it is the success of the intervention in overcoming dependence that matters.

Key points
- Motivation to stop smoking can be assessed with simple questions
- Once a decision to quit is made, success is determined more by the degree of dependence than the level of motivation
- Simple questions can identify heavily dependent smokers
- For high dependence, higher strength nicotine products may help

Competing interests: RW has done paid research and consultancy for, and received travel funds and hospitality from, manufacturers of smoking cessation products, including nicotine replacement therapies and Zyban. See chapter 1 for the series editor's competing interests.

Dependence and dose of nicotine in treatment
- The nicotine dose should be guided by measures of dependence
- The higher strength forms of nicotine replacement are particularly recommended for high dependence smokers
- For nicotine therapy, high dependence smoking is typically considered to be at least 15-20 cigarettes a day and/or smoking within 30 minutes of waking

Nicotine therapy will be covered in a later article in this series

---

Estimated prevalence of selected indices of motivation to stop smoking

Index	% of smokers
Would like to stop smoking for good	70
Intend to stop smoking in next 12 months	46
Made an attempt to stop in a given year	30
Used medication to aid cessation in a given year*	8
Attended smokers clinic or followed behavioural support programme†	2

*Based on surveys showing that 30% of smokers make a quit attempt each year and that in 25% of quit attempts medication is used.
†Based on figures from attendance in 2001 at NHS cessation clinics.

Do you want to stop smoking for good?	No/Yes
Are you interested in making a serious attempt to stop in the near future?	No/Yes
Are you interested in receiving help with your quit attempt?	No/Yes

Simple qualitative test of motivation to stop smoking. A "yes" response to all questions suggests that behavioural support and/or medication should be offered

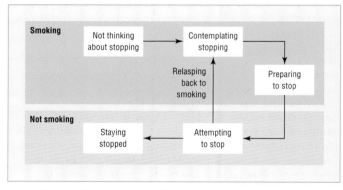

Stages of change in process of stopping smoking. Adapted from Prochaska et al. *Clin Chest Med* 1991;12:727-35

Further reading
- Kozlowski LT, Porter CQ, Orleans CT, Pope MA, Heatherton T. Predicting smoking cessation with self-reported measures of nicotine dependence: FTQ, FTND, and HSI. *Drug Alcohol Depend* 1994;34:211-6.
- National Institute for Clinical Excellence. *Technology appraisal guidance No 38. Nicotine replacement therapy (NRT) and bupropion for smoking cessation.* London: NICE, 2002.
- Sutton S. Back to the drawing board? A review of applications of the transtheoretical model to substance use. *Addiction* 2001;96:175-86.

4 Use of simple advice and behavioural support

Tim Coleman

The most effective methods of helping smokers to quit smoking combine pharmacotherapy (such as nicotine or bupropion) with advice and behavioural support. These two components contribute about equally to the success of the intervention. Doctors and other health professionals should therefore be familiar with what these strategies offer, encourage smokers to use them, and be able at least to provide simple advice and behavioural support to smokers. They also need to be familiar with other sources of support, such as written materials, telephone helplines, and strategies for preventing relapses. This chapter focuses on non-pharmacological interventions.

Brief advice

The Cochrane Tobacco Addiction Group defines brief advice against smoking as "verbal instructions to stop smoking with or without added information about the harmful effects of smoking." All the published guidelines on managing smoking cessation recommend that all health professionals should give simple brief advice routinely to all smokers whom they encounter. The success rate of brief advice is modest, achieving cessation in about 1 in 40 smokers, but brief advice is one of the most cost effective interventions in medicine. The previous article in this series gave tips on how to take account of smokers' motivation to stop, but the key point is that only one or two minutes are needed for effective brief advice to be delivered in routine consultations.

Advice along these lines is probably most effective in smokers with established smoking related disease. It is also more effective if more time is spent discussing smoking and cessation and if a follow up visit is arranged to review progress. More intensive advice (taking more than 20 minutes at the initial consultation), inclusion of additional methods of reinforcing advice (such as self help manuals, videos, or CD Roms and showing smokers' their exhaled carbon monoxide levels), and follow up can increase success rates by a factor of 1.4. Again, the cost effectiveness of these more intensive interventions is extremely high—higher than many of the interventions provided routinely in primary or secondary care. The case is therefore strong to integrate simple advice into all health consultations with smokers and to offer more intensive advice and follow up to smokers who are motivated to quit.

Behavioural support

Intensive behavioural support provided outside routine clinical care by appropriately trained smoking cessation counsellors is the most effective non-pharmacological intervention for smokers who are strongly motivated to quit. Meta-analyses of trials have shown that about 1 in 13 smokers who are motivated enough to attend individual counselling from a smoking cessation counsellor are likely to quit as a result of this. Different approaches to counselling based on various psychological models have been studied, but no one type of intensive behavioural support is clearly more effective than any other. Behavioural support usually involves a review of patients' smoking histories and their motivation to quit, with smokers being helped to identify situations where they might have a

Suggested phrasing for giving brief advice to smokers

- "The best thing you can do for your health is to stop smoking, and I would advise you to stop as soon as possible."
- "Tobacco is very addictive, so it can be very difficult to give up, and many people have to try several times before they succeed. Your chances of succeeding are much greater if you make use of counselling support, which I can arrange for you, and either nicotine replacement therapy or the antismoking drug Zyban [bupropion], which I can prescribe for you if you wish."
- "If you are ready to try to give up smoking now, then the best thing is to see a counsellor as soon as possible, and I can arrange that for you. If not, then I'd like you to take home this leaflet and read it, or ring the NHS smokers' helpline, to get further information."
- "The best thing is to get counselling from experts, but if this isn't possible, you should make sure that you have good information on the health effects of smoking and some tips on ways of stopping smoking and that you know where to turn for further help and support."
- "How do you feel about your smoking?"
- "How do you feel about tackling your smoking now?"

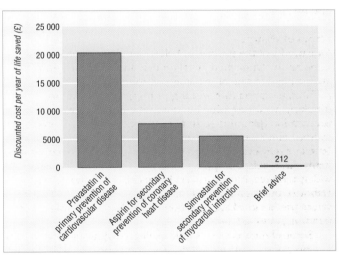

Cost effectiveness of brief advice versus common medical interventions

Measuring the level of carbon monoxide in smokers' exhaled air can motivate them to quit or be a useful tool in monitoring their progress with cessation

high risk of relapsing during a quit attempt; counsellors also encourage smokers to develop problem based strategies for dealing with these situations.

Intensive behavioural support is equally effective whether for an individual or on a group basis, but the latter is more cost effective (although not all smokers are willing to take part in a group). Moreover, in a group, smokers gain mutual support from other smokers who are trying to quit. Sessions are generally smoker oriented, and group facilitators, who manage 20 to 25 smokers simultaneously, ensure that smokers' key concerns about quitting are tackled.

Who should deliver these interventions?

All doctors and other health professionals should provide brief advice as a low intensity but routine intervention to all smokers who use their services. For smokers who do not wish to take up intensive behavioural support, doctors or other professionals should, where possible, also provide advice and follow up in primary and secondary care services; this should be provided either directly by the primary or secondary care clinician or by arrangement with another healthcare professional. Intensive support services need to be available to all smokers by referral. How to organise and deliver these services is discussed later in this series.

In the United Kingdom, smoking cessation services have now been established as part of a national initiative, and all health professionals should be able to refer smokers for behavioural support from a person who has specifically trained for this role. Any interested, trained health professional can be an effective smoking cessation counsellor, and those working for smoking cessation services in England come from varied clinical and non-clinical backgrounds.

Written self help materials and helplines

Self help materials that aim to promote smoking cessation are defined by the Cochrane Collaboration as "structured programming for smokers trying to quit without intensive contact from a therapist." This definition includes written leaflets, videos, and CD Roms. Giving smokers self help materials is more effective than doing nothing but is not as effective as simple advice. The effectiveness of self help materials may be improved by tailoring them to individual smokers' needs. Telephone helplines are widely available and provide a simple alternative means of providing low cost counselling or advice to motivated smokers, although they are also less effective than face to face advice from a health professional.

Complementary therapies

Complementary therapies have been advocated by some as effective cessation interventions, but little evidence exists to support their use. Acupuncture and related therapies such as acupressure have been found to be no more effective than placebo therapies. Similarly, although hypnotherapy is also provided in the belief that it can weaken the desire to smoke or can strengthen the will to stop, no convincing evidence exists that it works. Designing placebo care for randomised, controlled trials of complementary therapies is challenging, but without such trials no conclusions can be reached about the utility of complementary therapies in smoking cessation.

Strategies used in intensive behavioural support

- Review smoking history—number smoked per day, time of first cigarette in the day. Ask smoker to keep diary of activities that coincide with smoking
- Review smoking behaviour—past quit attempts, what helped, and reasons for failure
- Emphasise need for total abstinence
- Emphasise need to combat psychological and physical nicotine addiction, where appropriate
- Identify triggers to smoking and encourage smoker to develop strategies for countering these (for example, avoid places or activities associated with smoking)
- If relevant, encourage smoker to develop strategies for avoiding relapse when drinking alcohol
- Encourage appropriate action: set quit date, inform or enlist support of peer group or family, and prescribe nicotine addiction treatment
- Follow up to review progress and prescribe or issue nicotine addiction treatment

Adequate training in smoking cessation counselling is much more important than the discipline of the health professional providing that support

Written leaflets can also help people to stop smoking

Websites giving quitline information

- http://cancercontrol.cancer.gov/tcrb/quitlines.html (United States)
- www.ash.org.uk/html/quit/givingup.html (for guide to UK quitlines)
- www.asianquitline.org (UK, for Asians)
- www.quitnow.info.au/quitlineinfo.html (Australia)
- www.quit.org.nz (New Zealand)

The challenge for those who advocate complementary therapies in smoking cessation is to provide evidence for their effectiveness

Prevention of relapse

Most smokers who are trying to stop make several quit attempts before they succeed. Consequently, smokers have frequently been provided with treatments that health professionals believe will help smokers to sustain quit attempts and will help to prevent relapse. Recent American guidelines on smoking cessation recommended that when clinicians encounter a patient who has recently quit smoking they should reinforce the patient's decision to quit and help the patient to resolve any residual problems.

Combination with pharmacotherapy

All the evidence on the combination of non-pharmacological and pharmacological interventions indicates that the effects multiply rather than add together. Therefore the effectiveness of all non-pharmacological therapy is increased substantially by pharmacotherapy, and the more intensive the non-pharmacological support, the greater the extent of that increase. It is therefore important that non-pharmacological interventions are recognised as equal contributors to the overall success of smoking cessation interventions, which can achieve up to 20% success with any quit attempt, and that they are not discarded as inferior or irrelevant alternatives to drug treatment. The provision of non-pharmacological interventions, ranging from simple advice to intensive behavioural support, needs to become a routine component of healthcare delivery to smokers.

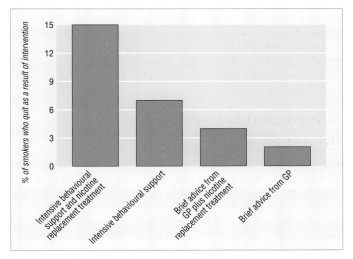

Comparison of effective smoking cessation interventions: percentage of smokers who quit as a result of the intervention. Adapted from Raw et al. *Thorax.* 1998;53(suppl 5, part 1):S1-19

Further reading

- Silagy C, Stead LF. Physician advice for smoking cessation. *Cochrane Database Syst Rev* 2003;(2):CD000165.
- Lancaster T, Stead LF. Individual behavioural counselling for smoking cessation. *Cochrane Database Syst Rev* 2003;(2):CD001292.
- Lancaster T, Stead LF. Self-help interventions for smoking cessation. *Cochrane Database Syst Rev* 2003;(2):CD001118.
- Stead LF, Lancaster T. Group behaviour therapy programmes for smoking cessation. *Cochrane Database Syst Rev* 2003;(2):CD001007.
- Stead LF, Lancaster T, Perera R. Telephone counselling for smoking cessation. *Cochrane Database Syst Rev* 2003;(2):CD002850.

Key points

- Simple advice to give up smoking is one of the most cost effective interventions in medicine
- Doctors and other health professionals should routinely give brief, non-judgmental advice to stop smoking to all smokers they see
- Self help materials such as leaflets, videos, or helplines provide additional support
- Intensive behavioural support from a trained counsellor is the most effective non-drug treatment for smokers
- Behavioural support is equally effective for groups and individuals
- The most effective interventions combine behavioural support with drug treatment
- Therapy that combines drug treatment with the level of behavioural support most acceptable to the smoker should be routinely available to all smokers

Competing interests: TC has been paid for speaking at a conference by GlaxoSmithKline, a drug company that manufactures treatments for nicotine addiction; he has also done consultancy work on one occasion for Pharmacia. See chapter 1 for the series editor's competing interests.

5 Nicotine replacement therapy

Andrew Molyneux

Although products for nicotine replacement therapy (NRT) have been available for over 20 years, they have been excluded until recently from state or insurance based health service provision in the United Kingdom and many other countries. They have therefore not been widely prescribed by doctors who help smokers wanting to quit. Recent changes in funding policy in the United Kingdom and new guidance from the National Institute for Clinical Excellence (which covers England and Wales) mean that NRT products can and should now be made available to all smokers who want to stop smoking.

Like other pharmacological interventions for helping smokers to quit (see the next chapter), NRT is most effective when used in conjunction with behavioural and other types of non-pharmacological cessation interventions.

Mechanism of action

The main mode of action of NRT is thought to be the stimulation of nicotinic receptors in the ventral tegmental area of the brain and the consequent release of dopamine in the nucleus accumbens. This and other peripheral actions of nicotine lead to a reduction in nicotine withdrawal symptoms in regular smokers who abstain from smoking.

NRT may also provide a coping mechanism, making cigarettes less rewarding to smoke. It does not completely eliminate the symptoms of withdrawal, however, possibly because none of the available nicotine delivery systems reproduce the rapid and high levels of arterial nicotine achieved when cigarette smoke is inhaled.

All the available medicinal nicotine products rely on systemic venous absorption and do not therefore achieve such rapid systemic arterial delivery. It takes a few seconds for high doses of nicotine from a cigarette to reach the brain; medicinal products achieve lower levels over a period of minutes (for nasal spray or oral products such as gum, inhalator, sublingual tablet, or lozenge) and hours (for transdermal patches).

Evidence for effectiveness

The most recent Cochrane reviews suggest that NRT leads to a near doubling of cessation rates achieved by non-pharmacological intervention, irrespective of the level of that intervention.

NRT will therefore increase the chance of success with any quit attempt but is most effective when combined with intensive behavioural support.

No evidence exists that NRT is any more or less effective in any specific subgroups of smokers, such as those in hospital or presenting with a smoking related disease. The effectiveness of NRT in adolescents and children who smoke has not been established, though studies are in progress.

Who should receive NRT?

Nicotine replacement therapy, preferably in conjunction with behavioural support (see the previous chapter), should generally be offered to any regular cigarette smoker

This article outlines the mechanism of action of nicotine replacement therapy (NRT), the evidence for its effectiveness, and how and when NRT products can be used

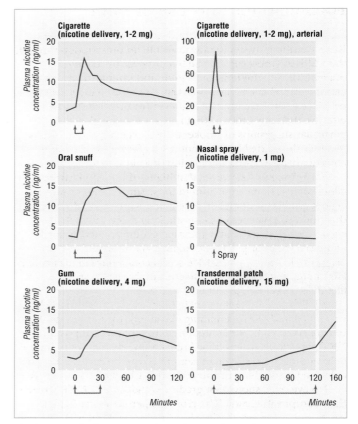

Rise in blood nicotine concentrations after smoking a cigarette and after using different NRT products (after overnight abstinence from cigarettes). Values are for venous blood, except where shown. Adapted from Henningfield JE. *N Engl J Med* 1995;333:1196-203

Proportion of smokers abstaining from smoking long term, by cessation intervention. Adapted from West et al, 2000*

Intervention	Long term abstinence (%)
No intervention (willpower alone)	3
Brief, opportunistic advice from doctor to stop	5
Plus NRT	10
Intensive support from specialist	10
Plus NRT	18

*See Further Reading box

prepared to make a quit attempt. NRT is relatively unlikely to help smokers who are not motivated to quit or do not experience or expect to experience nicotine withdrawal symptoms. Any healthcare professionals can assess these characteristics in the following ways:

● Motivation to quit: smokers should be asked whether they would like to stop smoking. Those willing to stop within the next 30 days should set a quit date and their dependence should be assessed.

● Dependence: smokers should be asked whether they have tried to quit smoking before, whether they experienced symptoms of nicotine withdrawal, and whether they anticipate these symptoms in a future quit attempt.

Formulations and use of NRT

Six NRT formulations are currently available. In the United Kingdom, all of these are now available on prescription through the NHS and most can also be bought over the counter at pharmacies. In addition, patch, gum, and lozenge formulations are on general sale in supermarkets and other outlets. As little evidence exists that any one of these formulations is more effective than any other or that any is more effective in particular subgroups of smokers, the choice of product should generally be guided by the smoker's preference and clinical considerations relating to duration of action.

Evidence exists, however, that higher dose gum is more effective than lower dose gum in those smoking 20 or more cigarettes a day, that higher dose patches are more effective than low dose patches in those smoking more than 10 cigarettes a day, and that combining products (such as patch and nasal spray, or patch and inhalator) is more effective than using single agents alone. NRT, and nicotine gum in particular, has also been shown to help to control the weight gain commonly experienced after cessation.

NRT should be prescribed in blocks, usually of two weeks, be continued in those maintaining abstinence from cigarettes for a total of six to eight weeks, and then discontinued. If possible, NRT prescriptions should be linked to the delivery of follow up behavioural support. The prescriptions can be issued through delegated prescribing by nurses or other health professionals.

No evidence shows that gradual withdrawal of NRT is better than abrupt withdrawal. The risk of dependence on NRT is small, and only a small minority of patients (about 5%) who quit successfully continue to use medicinal nicotine regularly in the longer term.

Studies investigating the use of NRT to help smokers to abstain from smoking for certain periods (for example, at work or in a public place) or to reduce the number of cigarettes they smoke each day are in progress.

Safety of NRT

Obtaining nicotine from NRT is considerably safer than doing so from cigarettes, as the patient is not exposed to any of the many harmful products of tobacco combustion.

Long term use of NRT is not thought to be associated with any serious harmful effects. Concerns over the safety of NRT in circumstances in which nicotine might be harmful—such as in pregnancy, cardiovascular disease, or in adolescents—therefore need to be considered in relation to the safety of the likely alternative, which is continued intake of nicotine from cigarettes.

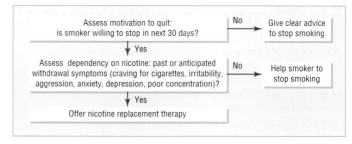

Decision pathway for giving nicotine replacement therapy

NRT formulations and their availability

Transdermal patch—On general sale,* at pharmacies, and on prescription
Gum—On general sale,* at pharmacies, and on prescription
Nasal spray—At pharmacies and on prescription
Inhaler—At pharmacies and on prescription
Sublingual tablet—At pharmacies and on prescription
Lozenge—On general sale,* at pharmacies, and on prescription

*In supermarkets and other outlets

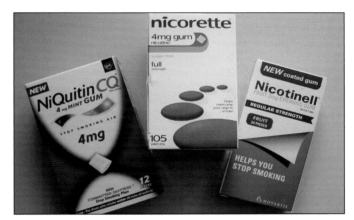

Nicotine gum products

Smokers should be advised not to smoke while using NRT products

---

Prescribing details for NRT formulations

Formulation (dose)	Use
Patch (16 h patch: 15, 10, or 5 mg; 24 patch: 21, 14, or 7 mg)	One daily on clean, unbroken skin; remove before bed (16 h patch) or next morning (24 h); new patch, fresh site
Gum (2 or 4 mg per piece)	Chew gum until taste is strong, then rest gum between gum and cheek; chew again when taste has faded
Inhalator (10 mg per cartridge)	Inhale as required
Sublingual tablet (2 or 4 mg per piece)	Rest under tongue until dissolved
Lozenge (1, 2, or 4 mg per piece)	Place between gum and cheek and allow to dissolve
Nasal spray (10 mg/ml, 0.5 mg per spray)	One spray each nostril as required

Side effects for all formulations: sore throat, hiccups, indigestion, nausea, headache, palpitations (but without hiccups for the inhalator and plus itching, erythma, and rash for patches).

Pregnancy and breast feeding

Smoking during and after pregnancy poses a serious risk to the health of both mother and baby. NRT may also have adverse effects on placental function and fetal development, but although the magnitude of these pure nicotine effects in humans is uncertain, the likelihood is that obtaining nicotine from cigarette smoke is far more harmful.

Complete avoidance of all nicotine should therefore be the objective in pregnancy and breast feeding, and 30% of pregnant women succeed in stopping smoking during pregnancy without pharmacological support. However, for those who do not succeed, or have previously failed in an attempt to quit, the use of NRT to support smoking cessation in pregnancy is justifiable in relation to the risk of continued smoking. Pregnant or breast feeding women who make an informed choice to try NRT should probably be advised to use shorter acting products to minimise fetal exposure to nicotine overnight.

Cardiovascular disease

Nicotine replacement therapy is safe in smokers with stable cardiovascular disease. In acute cardiovascular conditions, such as unstable angina, acute myocardial infarction, or stroke, NRT should be used with caution because nicotine is a vasoconstrictor. However, as medicinal nicotine is unlikely to be more harmful in this context than continued intake of nicotine (and the associated tar, carbon monoxide, and other products) from cigarettes, it is appropriate to offer NRT to help in smoking cessation in patients with acute cardiovascular disease who continue to smoke. In these circumstances it is probably advisable to use rapidly reversible preparations—such as gum, inhalator, nasal spray, or lozenge—as absorption of nicotine ceases when the product is withdrawn; after removal of a transdermal patch, however, the skin can continue to absorb nicotine slowly from the skin for some time.

Young smokers

Most adult smokers established their smoking habit as children. Even in adolescence, many smokers are addicted to nicotine and would like to stop smoking. Over two thirds of adolescent smokers have tried to stop, and failed. Although no randomised controlled trials of the effectiveness of NRT in young smokers have been published, several NRT products are licensed for use in smokers aged under 18, on medical advice. In addition, the recent National Institute for Clinical Excellence guidance on NRT suggests that smokers under 18 who want to quit using NRT should discuss this with a relevant healthcare professional. Until further evidence arises to the contrary, it therefore seems reasonable to use NRT in adolescent smokers who are motivated to quit and show evidence of nicotine dependence.

Competing interests: AM has received research funding and been reimbursed for attending conferences by Pharmacia, a manufacturer of NRT. He has also received speaking fees and been reimbursed for attending a conference by GlaxoSmithKline, which manufactures bupropion and NRT. See chapter 1 for the series editor's competing interests.

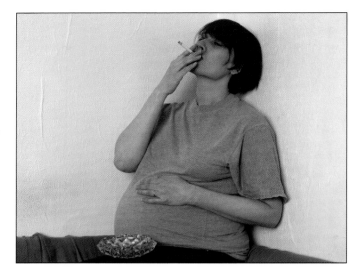

Key points

- Nicotine replacement therapy is an effective aid to smoking cessation
- Smokers who are motivated to quit and are dependent on nicotine should be offered NRT
- The choice of NRT product should normally be guided by the patient's preference
- NRT should be prescribed for six to eight weeks, in blocks of up to two weeks, contingent on continued abstinence
- Obtaining nicotine from NRT is considerably safer than smoking
- NRT is safe in stable cardiac disease, but caution is needed in unstable, acute cardiovascular disease, pregnancy, or breast feeding, or in those aged under 18

Further reading

- Silagy C, Mant D, Fowler G, Lancaster T. Nicotine replacement therapy for smoking cessation. *Cochrane Database Syst Rev* 2000;CD000146.
- Tobacco Advisory Group of the Royal College of Physicians. *Nicotine addiction in Britain*. RCP: London, 2000.
- West R, McNeill A, Raw M. Smoking cessation guidelines for health professionals: an update. *Thorax* 2000;55:987-99.
- Fiore MC, Bailey WC, Cohen SJ, Dorfman SF, Fox BJ, Goldstein MG, et al. A clinical practice guideline for treating tobacco use and dependence. *JAMA* 2000;283:3244-54.

The photo of the pregnant woman is with permission from Faye Norman/SPL.

6 Bupropion and other non-nicotine pharmacotherapies

Elin Roddy

Although nicotine replacement has been the first line drug treatment for smoking cessation for many years, other drugs of proved efficacy are also now available. Foremost among these is bupropion (marketed as Zyban). Bupropion was developed and initially introduced in the United States as an antidepressant but was subsequently noted to reduce the desire to smoke cigarettes and shown in clinical trials to be effective in smoking cessation.

Mechanism of action

Bupropion is an atypical antidepressant structurally similar to diethylpropion, an appetite suppressant. The mechanism of the antidepressant effect of bupropion is not fully understood, but bupropion inhibits reuptake of dopamine, noradrenaline, and serotonin in the central nervous system, is a non-competitive nicotine receptor antagonist, and at high concentrations inhibits the firing of noradrenergic neurons in the locus caeruleus.

It is not clear which of these effects accounts for the antismoking activity of the drug, but inhibition of the reductions in levels of dopamine and noradrenaline levels in the central nervous system that occur in nicotine withdrawal is likely to be important. The antismoking effect of bupropion does not seem to be related to the antidepressant effect as bupropion is equally effective as a smoking cessation therapy in smokers with and without depression.

Evidence for effectiveness

When given in association with intensive behavioural support, bupropion is as effective as nicotine replacement therapy (NRT), and like NRT, leads to a near doubling of the smoking cessation rate, achieving long term abstinence in 19% of smokers who use it to quit.

The effectiveness of bupropion in conjunction with less intensive levels of behavioural support has not been tested in clinical trials. Like NRT, however, bupropion therapy probably increases the chance of success with any quit attempt but is most effective when combined with intensive behavioural support. No evidence suggests that bupropion is any more or less effective in any specific subgroups of smokers, such as those in hospital or those with a smoking related disease.

Bupropion also seems to attenuate the weight gain that often occurs after quitting. More prolonged use of bupropion (beyond the recommended eight weeks) seems to confer further protection against relapse.

Using bupropion

Dose
Bupropion is marketed in the United Kingdom as an oral prolonged release 150 mg tablet. An eight week course of treatment is recommended and costs about £86 ($143; €123). Smokers should start taking bupropion one week before their intended quit date. A reduced dose—that is, one tablet daily—is recommended in elderly people and those with liver or renal impairment.

Bupropion is the only non-nicotine drug licensed for use in smoking cessation in the United Kingdom and the European Union; it became available for use in 2000

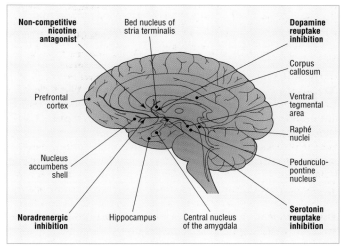

Effects of bupropion on the central nervous system

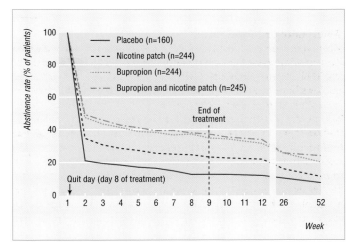

Abstinence from smoking in relation to sustained release bupropion or nicotine patch, or both. Adapted from Jorenby et al. *N Engl J Med* 1999;340:685-91

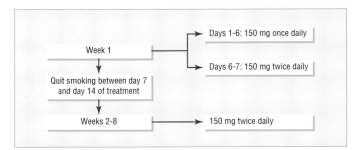

Dose regimen for bupropion

15

Unwanted effects

The most serious adverse effect of bupropion is seizure, which affects an estimated 1 in 1000 users. More common side effects include dry mouth, insomnia, skin rash, pruritus, and hypersensitivity. Rarely the drug may cause a reaction resembling serum sickness.

Contraindications and precautions

Bupropion is contraindicated in patients with current or past epilepsy. It should also be used with extreme caution in patients with conditions predisposing to a low threshold for seizure —history of head trauma, alcohol misuse, diabetes treated with hypoglycaemic agents or insulin—and in patients taking drugs that lower the seizure threshold (for example, theophylline, antipsychotics, antidepressants, and systemic corticosteroids).

Bupropion is also contraindicated in patients with a history of anorexia nervosa and bulimia, severe hepatic necrosis, or bipolar disorder.

Pharmacokinetics and interactions

Bupropion reaches a peak plasma concentration three hours after oral administration, with steady state concentration reached within eight days. It has a half life of 20 hours and is metabolised in the liver by cytochrome p450.

Power of the press

- The use of bupropion has been inhibited in the United Kingdom by a series of articles in national newspapers soon after the drug was launched
- These implicated bupropion in some serious adverse effects, including death, in a number of cases
- Post-marketing surveillance has since shown that serious adverse events are rare with bupropion, occurring at about half the average reported rate for new drugs in Britain

Bupropion should not be used with a monoamine oxidase inhibitor, and at least 14 days should elapse between stopping such treatment and starting bupropion

Bupropion interacts with a number of commonly used drugs, including some antidepressants, type 1c antiarrhythmics, and antipsychotics

Interactions of bupropion

Drug	Mechanism of interaction	Action required
Antidepressants (desipramine, fluoxetine)	Prolongs action of drugs metabolised by cytochrome p450 (CTP2D6)	Start these drugs at low end of dose range in patients already taking bupropion. Decrease dose of ongoing treatment with these drugs if patient starts bupropion
Antipsychotics (risperidone, thioridazine)		
Type 1c antiarrhythmics (propafenone, flecainide)		
β blockers (metoprolol)		
Antiepileptics (carbamazepine, phenobarbitone, phenytoin)	Metabolism of bupropion induced	Bupropion dose increase not recommended*
Levodopa	Limited clinical data suggest higher incidence of adverse events	Give bupropion with caution to patients receiving levodopa
MAOIs (including moclobemide)	Avoid using bupropion for two weeks after MAOIs	
Ritonavir	Increased plasma bupropion concentration; risk of increased toxicity	Avoid concomitant use

MAOI=mono amine oxidase inhibitor.
*Bupropion contraindicated in epilepsy.

Use with NRT

One study has suggested that combined nicotine patch therapy and bupropion may produce higher quit rates than nicotine patches alone. Combination therapy may therefore be recommended to patients attending specialist cessation clinics who find it difficult to quit using a single pharmacotherapy. Monitoring for hypertension is recommended when combined therapy is used.

Special groups

Chronic obstructive pulmonary disease—Smoking cessation is the most important intervention in this disease. Bupropion has been shown to be effective and well tolerated in this group of patients.

Ischaemic heart disease—Smoking cessation is one of the most important interventions in this disease. Bupropion is not contraindicated or subject to caution except in diabetic patients treated with hypoglycaemic agents or insulin (caution) or in patients taking propafenone or flecainide (dose reduction of antiarrhythmics advised).

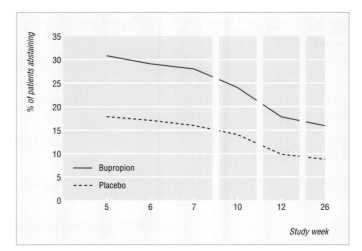

Long term abstinence from smoking in patients with chronic obstructive pulmonary disease, after treatment with bupropion. Adapted from Tashkin et al. *Lancet* 2001;357:1571-5

Pregnant women—No trials of bupropion have been done in pregnant women. Bupropion is therefore not recommended for use in pregnancy.

Other antidepressants

Nortriptyline, a tricyclic antidepressant with mostly noradrenergic properties and a small amount of dopaminergic activity, is also effective in cessation therapy, and although few clinical trials have been done, these suggest an effect of similar magnitude to that of bupropion. Again, this effect seems to be independent of the presence of depressive symptoms.

Several other antidepressants have been used in smoking cessation including imipramine, doxepin, venlafaxine, fluoxetine, and the reversible monoamine oxidase inhibitor moclobemide. The latter may be effective in some patients, but the effectiveness of other therapies is unproved.

Other pharmacotherapies

Clonidine is an α noradrenergic agonist that suppresses sympathetic activity and has been used for hypertension and to reduce withdrawal symptoms associated with misuse of alcohol and opiates. Both in its oral and low dose patch formulation, clonidine increased smoking cessation in eight out of nine trials, but the drug is associated with serious side effects, including sedation and postural hypotension. Clonidine is therefore probably best reserved for smokers who cannot or do not wish to use NRT, bupropion, or nortriptyline.

Mecamylamine is a nicotinic antagonist originally used to decrease cholinergic activity and thus reduce blood pressure. It blocks the effects of nicotine but does not precipitate withdrawal symptoms. Two trials have suggested that a low dose mecamylamine patch combined with a nicotine patch was superior to placebo, but a recent multicentre trial has failed to show efficacy.

Sensory replacement therapy could be useful for the many smokers who report missing the sensory aspects of smoking. Sensory effects of smoking are important in reinforcing smoking behaviour, and loss of these effects may contribute to relapse. Two inhalers containing ascorbic acid or citric acid have been tested, and both increased rates of short term cessation. Further testing of these adjuncts to NRT or other non-nicotine therapies is warranted, but neither of these treatments is currently used routinely in specialist cessation clinics.

Competing interests: ER has been reimbursed by GlaxoSmithKline, the manufacturer of bupropion, for attending one international meeting and has attended educational events sponsored by Pharmacia, the manufacturer of Nicorette. See chapter 1 for the series editor's competing interests.

No trials of bupropion have been done in smokers aged under 18, and the drug is not licensed or recommended for smoking cessation in this age group

---

Non-nicotine therapies for smoking cessation

Proved effective—Bupropion, clonidine, nortriptyline
Possibly effective—Noradrenergic antidepressants, monoamine oxidase inhibitors, mecamylamine plus nicotine replacement therapy, sensory replacement
Ineffective or insufficient evidence—Anorectics, benzodiazepines, β blockers, buspirone, caffeine, ephedrine, cimetidine, dextrose, lobeline, naltrexone, ondansetron, phenylpropanolamine, silver acetate, stimulants, selective serotonin reuptake inhibitors

---

Key points

- NRT is the treatment of choice, but non-nicotine drugs are also available as an alternative
- Bupropion is the most commonly used non-nicotine treatment
- Bupropion is generally safe and well tolerated
- Bupropion is as effective as NRT and doubles quit rates when given alongside intensive behavioural support
- Bupropion must not be given to patients at increased risk of seizures
- Nortriptyline has been less widely studied, but its effectiveness seems similar to that of bupropion
- Any risks associated with these therapies are likely to be much less serious than the risks from continued smoking

---

Further reading

- Antidepressants for smoking cessation. *Cochrane Database Syst Rev* 2003;(3):CD000031
- Royal College of Physicians of London. *Nicotine addiction in Britain.* London: RCP, 2000.
- Hurt RD, Sachs DPL, Glover ED, Offord KP, Johnston JA, Dale LC, et al. A comparison of sustained-release bupropion and placebo for smoking cessation. *N Engl J Med* 1997;337:1195-202.

Elin Roddy is clinical research fellow at the University of Nottingham in the division of respiratory medicine at City Hospital, Nottingham.

7   Special groups of smokers

Tim Coleman

Earlier articles in this series have provided general guidance on delivering smoking cessation interventions. This chapter investigates issues relevant to several special groups of smokers.

Pregnant women

In the United Kingdom over a quarter of pregnant women who smoke continue to do so during pregnancy. These women tend to be young, single, of lower educational achievement, and in manual occupations. If they have a partner, their partner is also more likely to smoke. Smoking has substantial adverse effects on the unborn child, including growth retardation, preterm birth, miscarriage, and perinatal mortality. Most of this harm is probably caused by toxins in cigarette smoke, such as carbon monoxide, nicotine, cyanide, cadmium, and lead. Nicotine itself may cause harm, however, through placental vasoconstriction and possible developmental effects on the fetus.

Ideally, women should stop smoking before getting pregnant. In practice, however, few do, and it is pregnancy itself that seems to be the key motivator to stop. About a quarter of women who smoke manage to stop for at least part of their pregnancy, mostly within the first trimester, but most of these start smoking again after their child is born.

Most pregnant women (80% in UK surveys) accept that stopping smoking is the most important lifestyle change that they can make during pregnancy, and consequently most women will be receptive to discussion of their smoking and the possibility of stopping. Those who continue to smoke, however, tend to hold rather different views from those who give up—for example, only about 30% of those who continue to smoke believe that smoking during pregnancy is "very dangerous" to their baby, compared with 80% of those who quit. It is, therefore, particularly important that health professionals tailor their message to the perceptions and beliefs of smokers in different stages of pregnancy.

Evidence based cessation interventions

Behavioural interventions
The effectiveness of brief interventions by different health professionals is not as clearly established for pregnant smokers as for non-pregnant smokers, but some form of intervention is clearly necessary to prompt cessation. However, intensive cessation programmes delivered to pregnant women by specially trained staff outside routine antenatal care are of proved effectiveness in promoting cessation and in reducing low birth weight and preterm birth.

For every 100 pregnant women who are still smoking at the time of their booking an antenatal visit, about 10 will stop smoking with "usual care" and a further six or seven can be encouraged to stop as a result of formal cessation programmes. As the available trials have investigated the effects of varied programmes—with few common elements—it is difficult to draw conclusions about which facets of these are effective.

Pharmacotherapy
Ideally, to minimise potential adverse effects on the fetus, pregnant smokers should give up smoking without resort to pharmacotherapy. In practice, however, many do not. Thus, the

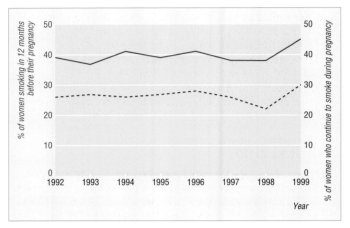

Prevalence of smoking in women before and during pregnancy, 1992-9. Adapted from Owen and Penn, 1999 (see Further Reading box)

Clinical issues to highlight or be aware of in relation to pregnant women who smoke*

Clinical issue	Reason
Women should stop smoking early in pregnancy if possible	Early quitting provides the greatest benefit to the fetus
Women can stop smoking any time during pregnancy	Fetus benefits even when women quit later in pregnancy
Emphasise the immediate benefits of stopping smoking	Both mother and baby will benefit very soon after stopping
Provide pregnancy related, motivational messages	These messages are associated with higher quit rates
Be alert to patients minimising or denying their smoking	Minimising or denying smoking is common among pregnant women who smoke

*Adapted from Fiore MC et al. *Smoking cessation. Clinical practice guideline No 18.* Rockville, MD: Department of Health and Human Services, Pubic Health Service, Agency for Health Care Policy and Research., 1998. (US AHCPR publication No 96-0692.)

Generally the more intensive the intervention the more effective it is; however, group based intensive interventions for pregnant women have tended to be poorly attended

---

Possible evidence based approach to cessation intervention in pregnancy

- Doctors and midwives should use their consultations to identify women who are motivated to try to stop
- They should then refer them for individual, intensive smoking cessation interventions
- These interventions can be delivered by specialist cessation services or any health professional with adequate time and training (see earlier chapter)

relative risks and benefits of pharmacotherapy need to be considered. As bupropion is specifically contraindicated in pregnancy, and other antidepressants are subject to special caution, the treatment of choice is nicotine replacement therapy (NRT). Any safety concerns about this treatment can be discounted by the fact that the alternative for most women is continued smoking and hence continued fetal exposure to nicotine and other toxins. To avoid unnecessary exposure of the fetus to nicotine it is probably advisable to avoid the longer acting NRT formulations, such as 24 hour transdermal patches.

However, although the only published placebo controlled trial of NRT in pregnancy showed a significant increase in birth weight in babies born to women who used NRT, it showed no effect on cessation. This is an area of high priority for further research.

Adolescents

In Britain, the proportion of young people starting to smoke has remained fairly stable over the past 20 years. In 1988, 8% of 11 to 15 year olds in England were regular smokers; by 1996 the proportion had increased to 13%, but since 1998 the figure has remained around 10%. As 80% of smokers start smoking as teenagers, the prevalence of smoking among teenagers has serious implications for public health. Young smokers are aware of the health risks of smoking and most would like to stop, but their attitudes towards their habit are more changeable than those of adult smokers. Although young smokers report smoking few cigarettes, many consider themselves to be addicted to tobacco and believe that stopping would be difficult. Young smokers are also more likely to drink alcohol or take illicit drugs.

Reducing smoking among young people presents a challenge for health professionals. Preventing uptake of smoking would result in the greatest population health gain, but the reasons why adolescents start smoking are many and complex (see chapter 2). Young people who have friends and family members who smoke are more likely to start themselves, and, for many young people, smoking is a social activity, with the first cigarette being provided by friends.

Many school based education campaigns aimed at preventing children from starting smoking have been studied, but the studies have shown mixed results. And as most of this work has been conducted in North America, the findings might not be completely generalisable to education systems in other countries. No evidence exists that campaigns involving giving information alone are effective, but where educational campaigns train young people to resist the social influences that encourage them to smoke, they can be effective.

"Social influence training" introduces young people to skills that, if used, reduce their likelihood of becoming regular smokers—for example, skills for refusing cigarettes when offered by peers. The best methods for preventing uptake of smoking by young people have yet to be discovered, and broad based prevention programmes that tackle the many factors involved in this have been advocated. One possible role for health professionals in such a universal strategy is to give brief advice reinforcing the health risks posed by smoking whenever young people present for health care.

Information is lacking about which smoking cessation interventions are effective for young people. Brief advice or behavioural counselling is likely to be effective, but this has yet to be proved. No randomised placebo controlled trials of NRT have been conducted among young smokers, and neither NRT nor bupropion is currently licensed for use in Britain in the under 16s. The best methods for delivering antismoking

Cessation interventions in pregnancy: recommendations and evidence*

Recommendation	Strength of evidence
Pregnant smokers should be strongly encouraged to stop throughout pregnancy; pregnant smokers should be offered intensive counselling treatment	A
Brief interventions (for example, brief advice from health professionals) should be used if more intensive interventions are not feasible	C
Motivational messages on the impact of smoking both on the pregnant woman and on the fetus should be given	C
Nicotine replacement therapy should be used during pregnancy if the benefits of using this (increased likelihood of cessation) outweigh the risks (from extra nicotine if women use the therapy and continue to smoke)	C

A = many well designed randomised controlled trials with a consistent pattern of findings. C = recommendation based on panel consensus in the absence of evidence from randomised controlled trials.
*Adapted from Fiore MC et al (details as for table, previous page).

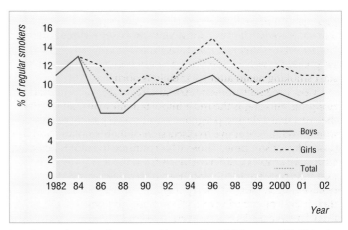

Prevalence of regular cigarette smoking in schoolchildren aged 11-15 in England, 1982-2002. Data from the Department of Health Statistics

Preventing uptake of smoking by young people

Factor to be tackled	Intervention
Influence of family members (parental smoking, sibling smoking, and family attitudes to smoking)	Local, community based initiatives running concurrently with school campaigns and media campaigns providing consistent messages
Peer influence	Social influence training (community or school based); media campaigns
School influence	School based social influence training; media campaigns
Relevance of media campaigns	Piloting or developmental work to refine messages for local populations
Changing young people's attitudes to smoking before they experiment with cigarettes	Develop campaigns aimed at children aged 4 to 8 years

Health professionals could consider becoming involved in school based, anti-tobacco education programmes that promote acquisition of social influence skills for young people

interventions to young people have also yet to be determined, as services designed for adults may not appeal to young smokers.

People with low income

Although the overall prevalence of smoking in the United Kingdom has decreased markedly over the past 30 years, little change has occurred among those living on low incomes. In the most deprived groups, smoking prevalence can be very high, reaching 90% among the homeless. The disparity in smoking prevalence between the most and least advantaged members of society is the single most important factor contributing to the gap in "healthy life expectancy" (amount of time that someone is expected to live in a healthy state) between these groups. As motivation to quit is fairly similar across social groups, poorer smokers cannot be blamed for failing to quit because they have lower motivation. As disadvantaged smokers tend to be more seriously addicted, however, there may be even greater justification for using pharmacotherapy in this group.

Ethnic minority groups

The prevalence of smoking varies greatly among different ethnic communities living in Britain. Bangladeshi, Black Caribbean, and Irish men and women have a higher than average prevalence of smoking, whereas fewer women from South Asian ethnic minority groups smoke compared with the general population. In the Bangladeshi population, the use of chewing tobacco is also common, with 19% of men and 26% of women using oral tobacco products.

Antismoking interventions described in earlier articles can all be used with smokers from ethnic minority groups. These interventions are probably all effective, but little research in the United Kingdom has specifically investigated whether the interventions differ in their effectiveness across ethnic groups. This has been investigated in the United States, however, where antismoking interventions were found to be of equal effectiveness across all racial groups. Health professionals need to bear in mind that some ethnic groups, especially Bangladeshis, may use tobacco in other harmful ways (for example, chewing) in addition to smoking it.

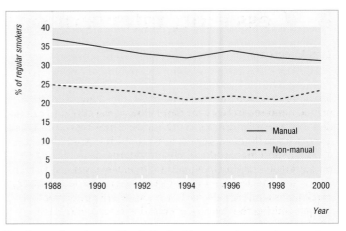

Prevalence of regular smoking in England by occupational socioeconomic group, 1988-2000. Data from general household survey

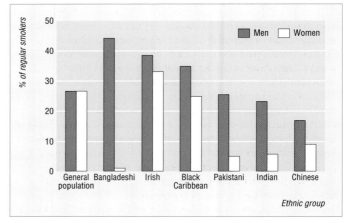

Prevalence of smoking in England, by ethnic minority group, 1999. Data from health survey for England

---

Further reading

- Preventing the uptake of smoking in young people. *Effective Health Care* 5(5). www.york.ac.uk/inst/crd/ehcb.htm
- Fiore MC. US public health service clinical practice guideline: treating tobacco use and dependence. *Respir Care* 2000;45:1200-62.
- Lumley J, Oliver S, Waters E. Interventions for promoting smoking cessation during pregnancy. *Cochrane Database Syst Rev* 2003;(3):CD 001055.
- Owen L, Penn G. *Smoking and pregnancy: a survey of knowledge, attitudes and behaviour, 1992-9.* London: Health Development Agency, 1999.
- Wisborg K, Henriksen TB, Jespersen LB, Secher NJ. Nicotine patches for pregnant smokers: a randomized controlled study. *Obstet Gynecol* 2000;96:967-71.

Key points

- Two thirds of women who stop smoking while pregnant restart afterwards
- Cessation programmes for pregnant women are effective; where these are available, health professionals must refer women to them
- Eighty per cent of adult smokers started smoking as teenagers, but effective methods of prevention or cessation for young people remain unknown
- Smoking is most common among poorer people, explaining much of the disparity in healthy life expectancy between the richest and poorest groups in Britain
- Patients from some ethnic groups are more likely to smoke than others; tobacco may also be chewed, especially among Bangladeshi people

---

The data for the last three graphs are from www.doh.gov.uk/public/ mainreport-smokingdrinkinganddruguse2002.pdf and www.statistics.gov.uk/lib2001/viewerchart5041.html and www.archive.official-documents.co.uk/document/doh/survey99/ hses-02.htm#gen19 respectively (accessed 15 December 2003).

Competing interests: TC has been paid for speaking at a conference by GlaxoSmithKline, a drug company that manufactures treatments for nicotine addiction; he has also done consultancy work on one occasion for Pharmacia. See chapter 1 for the series editor's competing interests.

8   Cessation interventions in routine health care

Tim Coleman

Smoking cessation interventions are widely underused in primary and secondary care despite being effective and easy to deliver (see earlier articles in this series). Smoking causes much greater harm than, say, hypertension (which is generally identified and managed entirely in primary care by health professionals working to agreed routine, systematic, and structured protocols), yet few primary healthcare teams manage smoking as methodically as they approach hypertension.

Maximising the delivery of cessation interventions to smokers wanting to quit can probably achieve more in terms of years of life saved and provide better value for money (see later chapter) than almost any other simple medical intervention.

Smoking as a vital sign

The first step towards developing a systematic approach for the management of smoking is to treat smoking as a "vital sign." To do this, health professionals must regularly inquire about patients' smoking status and have a methodical approach towards documenting and updating this in medical records. This information needs to be recorded in a prominent place so that it can be seen whenever medical records are accessed during consultations. In paper records, a summary card can be used, and, in electronic records, smoking status data should be lodged with other important summary information on a patient's health. Recording information where it is easily noticed prompts health professionals to raise the topic of smoking more frequently with patients.

The minimum information to record is whether the patient smokes and the date on which this was ascertained. It is also useful to record the average number of cigarettes smoked each day, not least because those who smoke more heavily are more likely to benefit from nicotine replacement therapy or bupropion therapy. Recording whether the smoker is interested in or motivated to try stopping smoking is also helpful: when health professionals raise the topic of smoking in future consultations, they can then tailor their messages to smokers' levels of motivation (see below).

Smokers' medical records should also be indexed so that they are readily identifiable and easy to retrieve. Without easy access to smokers' medical records, health professionals cannot effectively monitor their management of smoking. The simplest method for indexing smokers' medical records is to tag electronic records with one of the smoking status Read codes, but non-computerised general practices could use a simple card index. Monitoring longitudinal changes in patients' smoking behaviour and health professionals' delivery of cessation interventions is most appropriate in primary care because there is repeated contact between patients and primary healthcare teams. Health professionals can therefore treat smoking as a chronic disease, like asthma or diabetes.

The five "A"s approach

The five "A"s (ask, assess, advise, assist, arrange) summarise the role of health professionals in managing smoking. Health professionals are urged to ask all smokers about their smoking. Once smokers have been identified, it is important to assess

> **Managing smoking cessation needs to become a key part of routine practice for all clinicians. This article discusses strategies for incorporating effective antismoking interventions into routine clinical care**

Date............................	Smoker?	Yes	No
Number smoked per day.........................cigarettes/cigars			

Motivated to stop	Yes	No	Uncertain
Brief advice given	Yes	No	
NRT prescribed/recommended	Yes	No	Not applicable
Bupropion prescribed/recommended	Yes	No	Not applicable
Referred for intensive advice/ to cessation service	Yes	No	Not applicable

Example of record sheet for noting information on smoking status and intervention. The sheet can be inserted into paper records; computer templates enable a similar electronic record to be kept

Documentation of smoking in secondary care
- Smoking status, number of cigarettes smoked, and motivation to stop should be ascertained at all visits
- Electronic and paper records should be adapted to facilitate and promote the recording of this information

The five "A"s for antismoking interventions in routine care
- Ask about smoking at every opportunity
- Assess smokers' interest in stopping
- Advise against smoking
- Assist smokers to stop
- Arrange follow up

their interest in stopping smoking with an open question such as "how do you feel about your smoking?" It is important to ask sensitively as some smokers feel defensive when doctors raise the issue, and this can make it difficult to ascertain patients' true views.

All smokers, irrespective of their motivation to stop, need to be advised against smoking in a clear, personalised, and non-judgmental way. When smokers are clearly interested in stopping, health professionals should assist them to do so. Specific action will depend on the individual's circumstances, but, where appropriate, smokers should be encouraged to set a date for stopping completely, to plan for likely problems, and to enlist the support of family and friends. Health professionals should discuss the use of nicotine replacement therapy or bupropion with heavier smokers and prescribe either treatment if this is appropriate (see earlier chapter).

For smokers who want counselling and behavioural support, health professionals should also arrange for this to be provided, if possible from a specialist cessation service.

Implementing the approach

Success in integrating the five "A"s approach into routine clinical care will vary. In primary care, for example, patients visit doctors for a wide variety of reasons and general practitioners are, perhaps understandably, reluctant to raise the issue of smoking in all consultations..

Conversely, cardiologists and respiratory physicians will probably ask about smoking status in the vast majority of first consultations. Health professionals, therefore, should be encouraged to raise the issue of smoking with patients as often they believe is possible while recognising that discussing smoking is sometimes better left for subsequent consultations.

One way is to ensure that inquiring about smoking status and updating medical records is routine and systematic. If clinicians consider it inappropriate to raise the issue of smoking at all consultations, they should inquire and update records of smoking status at least annually. This gives clinicians the opportunity to select consultations in which to discuss smoking, taking into account patients' expectations of whether the issue should be tackled.

Health professionals often cite pressure of time, among other things, as a reason for not intervening against smoking more frequently. Smoking can be one of several important health issues that need tackling in a single, short consultation. The crucial difference between individual smokers is their motivation to stop. Smokers vary greatly in their motivation and, to make best use of limited time, health professionals should tailor their approach to the motivational level of the individual smoker (see chapter 3). As only about a fifth of smokers who attend general practitioners intend to try to stop smoking, it makes no sense for general practitioners to give all smokers they meet detailed information about how to stop. Non-motivated smokers need to be encouraged to change their attitudes to smoking before being urged to take action to quit.

Tailoring advice to motivation

Health professionals in both primary and secondary care can be encouraged to advise and assist smokers in a manner appropriate to their motivation to stop.

Primary care

"Help 2 Quit" (H2Q) is a smoking cessation service that encourages general practitioners to use their routine

Where counselling and behavioural support is not available, health professionals should consider providing follow up themselves or through another member of their team; this may be particularly convenient for smokers if pharmacotherapy for nicotine addiction is being prescribed and they cannot attend a specialist service

General practitioners tend to prefer to discuss smoking when patients present with smoking related problems, and they would generally avoid discussing smoking at all with some patients (for example, bereaved patients)

General practitioners' reasons for not giving smoking advice
- Patients are often not motivated to stop
- Patients often don't listen to advice
- Stopping smoking is often not a priority for smokers
- Lack of time
- Unwanted advice can annoy patients
- Difficult to impress on patients the importance of not smoking
- Do not know how to deal with smokers who are not motivated to stop

---

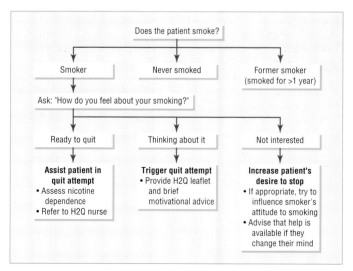

Opportunistic assessment of smokers' motivation: Help 2 Quit approach. Adapted from the Help 2 Quit cessation service, Shropshire County Primary Care Trust

consultations opportunistically to intervene against smoking. They are encouraged to identify each smoker's level of motivation for trying to quit as soon as possible after raising the issue of smoking with them, and to use this as a base for subsequent discussions on smoking. The primary objective of this method is to offer support to those who are ready to quit and improve their chances of success. H2Q uses a simplified version of the "stages of change" (see chapter 3) to tailor the intervention to the smoker. Although little empirical evidence exists to support the use of this approach, it fits well with clinical practice, including patients' expectations of how doctors should respond to their smoking.

Secondary care

In the H2Q approach, general practitioners are urged to treat more motivated and less motivated smokers differently: motivated smokers are given specific advice about quitting that would be inappropriate for those not interested in stopping. In Nottingham, midwives have developed a mechanism for incorporating inquiry and intervention into their routine work. When pregnant women attend their booking appointment for antenatal care, midwives use an algorithm to ask a series of questions about smoking.

As 80% of pregnant women believe that stopping smoking is the most important lifestyle change they can make to improve their babies' health, inquiring about smoking at all booking appointments is unlikely to upset many pregnant women. Midwives ask the women about smoking status, whether they live with smokers (including partners), and finally whether they or other smokers they live with are interested in quitting.

All smoking related data from manual records are entered into an electronic database for monitoring purposes. Midwives then respond to women in an appropriate way for their motivation level, and those who are interested in receiving extra support in quitting are referred to the local cessation service for behavioural counselling.

Monitoring management of smoking

All medical care systems sometimes experience some inertia or resistance to change. The fact that effective smoking cessation interventions have not been adopted into routine care despite their availability for over 20 years shows that this is especially true in relation to smoking cessation.

It is therefore important to monitor and audit the implementation and delivery of these services. This can be relatively simple when information about smoking is recorded electronically. For example, most general practice computer systems in the United Kingdom use Read codes, which allow clinicians to record data on smoking status simply and accurately.

Recently, new Read codes describing the three categories of smokers' motivation (and used by H2Q) have been approved, and these can now be used by any general practice computer system to record individual smokers' motivation to quit in medical records. Use of these Read codes and information on patient management from medical records provides a means for monitoring how primary care health professionals respond to smokers with differing levels of motivation.

> In the Help 2 Quit approach, general practitioners are urged to treat more motivated and less motivated smokers differently: motivated smokers are given specific advice about quitting that would be inappropriate for those not interested in stopping

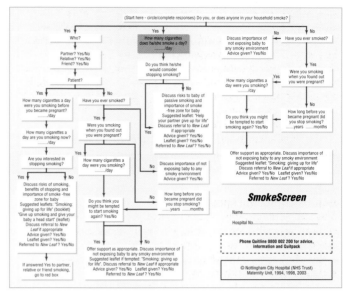

Flow chart for midwives inquiring about smoking at booking. From Nottingham City Hospital NHS Trust (see bmj.com for larger version)

Key points

- Smoking cessation interventions are simple, cheap, and effective but are not yet widely part of routine care
- Clinicians must develop and use routine and systematic approaches to inquiring about and recording patients' smoking status
- Cessation interventions need to be adapted to smokers' levels of motivation
- Cessation interventions need to be audited and monitored

Further reading

- Butler CC, Pill R, Stott NC. Qualitative study of patients' perceptions of doctors' advice to quit smoking: implications for opportunistic health promotion. *BMJ* 1998;316:1878-81.
- Coleman T, Murphy E, Cheater FC. Factors influencing discussions about smoking between general practitioners and patients who smoke: a qualitative study. *Br J Gen Pract* 2000;50:207-10.
- Rollnick SR, Mason P, Butler C. *Health behaviour change: a guide for practitioners.* London: Churchill Livingstone, 1999.
- West R, McNeill A, Raw M. Smoking cessation guidelines for health professionals: an update. *Thorax* 2000;55:987-99.

The adapted figure showing the "Help 2 Quit" approach is published with permission from K Lewis, and the flow chart for midwives with permission of Nottingham City Hospital (NHS Trust).

Competing interests: TC has been paid for speaking at a conference by GlaxoSmithKline, a drug company that manufactures treatments for nicotine addiction; he has also done consultancy work on one occasion for Pharmacia. See chapter 1 for the series editor's competing interests.

9   Setting up a cessation service

Penny Spice

In 1998, when the UK government announced the introduction of smoking cessation services throughout the NHS, few such services already existed. In most areas, therefore, the services had to be set up quickly and from scratch. This chapter reflects on some of the difficulties and challenges experienced in establishing and maintaining a cessation service, the Nottingham "New Leaf" service.

What is the likely demand?

Nottingham has a population of about 650 000—and therefore about 200 000 smokers. If (as expected from national data) 30% of these were to make a quit attempt in the same year, and all sought help from the cessation service, the demand would be overwhelming. In the event, however, initial demand rose fairly slowly. Some of the reasons for this slow start were:

● Smokers were initially suspicious of the new service. Many remarked that they expected to be "told off" about their smoking but were pleasantly surprised when encouraged instead to decide if the time was right for them to quit

● Health professionals were sceptical about the likely effectiveness of the service and had little understanding of what was offered

● There was also general suspicion, in an NHS based largely on a medical model, of services that relied on a health promotion approach, including client empowerment and behaviour change.

As a result, one of the major pressures in the early months was not the level of demand but the political pressure to meet high quit rate targets set by government.

Demand soon rose, however, as a result of various influences, such as the service's feedback of performance results to primary care teams. Although variable, the service currently deals each month with about 200 smokers who agree to set a quit date, of whom half are not smoking four weeks later.

Recruiting staff

Interest in joining the service was relatively low at first, though this changed considerably once New Leaf began to be known and respected.

It has since recruited staff from a wide range of backgrounds, including nursing, health promotion, community work, and counselling. Staff joining from a non-health background, however, have had to learn very quickly about working practices in the NHS and have at times been very frustrated over seemingly unnecessary hurdles of protocol and approval.

Although staff recruitment has become easier over time, retention has become increasingly difficult because the initial funding allocated by government expired after three years. Guarantees of continued salary support have subsequently tended to be short term and be delayed well into the financial year. Many staff move to other jobs because of the financial insecurity this causes.

Reasons for increasing use of New Leaf service

● Recommendations to others by smokers who have used the service
● Increasing familiarity, trust, and use of the service by health professionals
● Feedback of performance results to primary care team
● Spread of publicity through other partners, such as pharmacists
● Gradual incorporation of referral to cessation services into routine pathways and protocols
● Return of former clients who quit but started smoking again

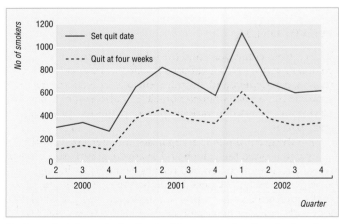

Numbers of smokers seen by New Leaf, by quarter, since launch of service in April 2000

Recruitment of staff from a wide range of backgrounds brings a rich mix of skills, experience, and perceptions into the service, with no established culture of "custom and practice"

Model of service provision

Within smoking cessation models there are three key approaches: high intensity with low coverage; medium intensity with medium coverage; and low intensity with high coverage.

Each of these has its relative advantages and disadvantages, and will reach different populations of smokers. New Leaf's policy from the outset was to try to provide services across the full range of these approaches, and to plan and recruit staff accordingly. Currently, 10 smoking cessation specialists and 15 sessional workers provide an intensive service, seeing about 4000 smokers a year. In addition, a network of 16 associate advisers based in primary and secondary care (many working part time for New Leaf) provide brief interventions as part of their normal work and offer support for former smokers who have completed the cessation programme. Overall, the service achieves an average quit rate, at four weeks, of 56%. In line with government guidance, it monitors the exhaled carbon monoxide levels of all clients.

Location

Two of the guiding principles for the service were that it should be accessible and that it should target smokers from disadvantaged areas.

To achieve these goals, New Leaf tried to ensure that its services were available at locations in the centres of local communities. It used deprivation indicators to identify disadvantaged areas of the city and the staff spent much time and effort finding venues in the right place, for the right amount of money, where staff would feel safe, that were accessible for people who used wheelchairs, and were on bus routes.

Thus New Leaf uses libraries, community centres, family centres, church halls, scout huts, a drop-in centre for homeless people, schools, prisons, colleges, and young people's centres. These are in addition to conventional healthcare sites, such as health centres, antenatal clinics, general practice surgeries, and hospitals.

Advertising

In the health community and the relevant statutory and voluntary sectors, New Leaf used briefings, presentations, reports, newsletters, and any other suitable internal means to promote the service wherever possible. It also ensured that the service was included in various "patient pathways," protocols, and policies.

For the general public, it organised an intensive publicity campaign around the launch and to advertise early successes of New Leaf. The campaign had various elements, including articles in local newspapers (including the free press); many radio appearances; flyers, posters, and credit cards; a New Leaf logo and phone number painted on a local bus; and displays and attendance at local health and community fairs.

Independence

It has proved important in Nottingham that the New Leaf cessation service was closely integrated into primary and secondary care while maintaining financial independence. This has ensured that funding allocated for smoking cessation has indeed been spent on the service and also encourages expertise and innovative ways of working. This autonomy also means that risks can be taken more easily and changes made more quickly than in larger administrations.

Three key approaches

High intensity with low coverage—"Closed" smoking cessation groups (usually for six to eight weeks), with follow up

Medium intensity with medium coverage—"Open" smoking cessation groups or clinics for smokers, usually on a one to one basis or with couples or families. This model allows the client to negotiate the length of time of the contact with the service, which may be shorter than the usual eight weeks

Low intensity with high coverage—Brief interventions, usually as part of another consultation or intervention

---

Groups or one-to-one services?

- The initial guidance on service development from the UK government focused primarily on group based, high intensity services
- This later changed to include "intermediate" services (interpreted to mean one to one sessions of shorter duration)
- New Leaf offered both services from the outset

In poor areas, smoking prevalence can be high, although people's motivation to quit is no lower than in more affluent areas

An effective way to advertise a new cessation service

Funding

Funding for cessation services is especially vulnerable to diversion into other services, but some measures can be taken to help to protect the service.

Funding must be "ring-fenced" or allocated specifically for cessation services. Cessation services must have challenging and auditable targets. The funding allocated for services must allow for the provision of more than just the bare minimum—there has to be capacity to develop and offer tailor made services for particular client groups with special needs. Funding also needs to be committed for the medium rather than short term to provide reasonable job security for staff.

It is important to give fundholders, through accurate and regular updates about the successes of the services, evidence about the services' effectiveness and efficiency, and to prove that they provide added value to what existed before or what would exist if they disappeared. Quantitative information about throughput, quit rates, relapse, loss to follow up, and developments to support smokers with special needs (such as pregnant women, young smokers, and hard to reach groups) is also important.

The annual budget for New Leaf in Nottingham for 2002-3 was £465 000 ($790 000; €677 000), serving a population of about 650 000. This level of funding has been adequate for the delivery of basic needs and to provide some support for development of new and special initiatives. Less than this would provide a basic service—that is, for well motivated and mobile smokers—but little more.

How long to establish a service?

In Nottingham it took over two years to establish an effective and efficient core service, and there is still a long way to go to meet the diverse range of smokers' needs. As the service develops, there are new discoveries and different ways of streamlining the existing systems, and a high quality service will always learn from mistakes, its staff, other services, and, most importantly, its clients.

Further reading

- Department of Health. *Smoking kills. A white paper on tobacco.* London: DoH, 1998.
- West R, McNeill A, Raw M. Smoking cessation guidelines for health professionals: an update. *Thorax* 2000;55:987-99.
- Department of Health. *NHS smoking cessation services: service and monitoring guidance 2001/2.* London: DoH, 2001.
- Department of Health. *National cancer plan.* London: DoH, 2000.
- Department of Health. *National service framework for coronary heart disease.* London: DoH, 2000.
- Department of Health. *The NHS plan.* London: DoH, 2000.

The photograph showing a run-down block of flats is published with permission from Matthew Butler/Rex.

Competing interests: See chapter 1 for the series editor's competing interests.

Why funding may be diverted from smoking cessation services
- Smoking cessation is a preventive intervention; other more immediate demands may be perceived to be more deserving or important
- Perception that smokers "choose" to smoke, so their addiction to smoking (and consequent disease) is not a medical problem and should not compete for medical funds
- Belief that smokers should pay for their own services, offsetting the cost against long term savings on cigarette purchase
- Smoking cessation therapy is behavioural so is not medical

Persuading fundholders to prioritise cessation services is vital to ensuring the future of the services

Challenges for smoking cessation services
- Strategy with employer and partners
- Staff recruitment
- Accommodation for offices and clinics
- Policies and protocols
- Evaluation methods
- Purchase of furniture, office equipment
- Design and printing of paperwork for administration, evaluation, information for clients
- Engagement and joint working with partners in primary and secondary care
- Full partnership with local pharmacists
- Publicity strategy
- Training programme for cessation staff
- Awareness raising and training programme for existing health, statutory, and voluntary sector workers
- Financial planning
- User feedback
- Follow up systems
- Joint working with health professionals and the voluntary sector to ensure continued support of former clients
- Synthesis within wider tobacco control agenda—for example, tobacco control strategy
- Regular reports and communication with the Department of Health, primary care trusts, local health services, colleagues in the statutory and voluntary sector
- Training for health professionals and workers from the statutory and voluntary sectors in how to give brief opportunistic smoking cessation advice
- Establishment of "special" services—for example, for pregnancy and family service, young people, smokers from deprived communities and excluded groups, ethnic minority communities, people with learning disabilities, homeless people, people with mental health problems
- Programme of monitoring and evaluation
- Supporting former clients

Key points
- Setting up a smoking cessation service is challenging but can be done quickly and effectively
- A service needs to be autonomous in terms of funding and overall administration
- There will be a substantial demand once it is established
- A service needs to be accessible, responsive, and adaptable
- Funding and autonomy need to be guaranteed for the medium term to ensure efficient staff recruitment and service development

10 Population strategies to prevent smoking

Konrad Jamrozik

Interventions targeted at individual smokers are only part of the much broader spectrum of strategies to reduce the prevalence of smoking. This article summarises the population strategies that can make substantial contributions to smoking cessation and help to prevent people from taking up smoking. Ten important initiatives are used or have been proposed for reducing tobacco use at population level. Nine initiatives are discussed here; the tenth (the use of proved treatments) is covered in previous articles in this series.

Public places and workplaces

Policies that ban smoking in public places are effective in reducing passive smoking among non-smokers generally. They also protect vulnerable groups such as children and infants, adults with cardiac or respiratory disease, and pregnant women against the adverse effects of environmental tobacco smoke. Smoke-free policies in public places also send a clear message to young people about non-smoking being the norm, and they reduce the numbers of adults that young people see smoking.

In the workplace, smoke-free policies lead to some staff quitting—typically about 4% of the workforce—and reduce daily consumption among continuing smokers. Each extension of a smoke-free policy to a setting in which smoking was previously permitted requires both careful consideration of public opinion and systematic planning for the change. It is good practice to offer existing smokers in an organisation help in quitting during the lead-up to the introduction of a smoke-free policy, but most of those who quit in response to the change do so without special help.

Support for smoke-free policies typically increases among smokers and non-smokers alike once the policies are introduced, and in the state of South Australia, for example, the introduction of smoke-free policies in restaurants and cafes indicates that such policies have no adverse economic impact.

Ten point plan for tobacco control

Issue and initiative	Importance
Public places and workplaces: comprehensive smoke-free policies	Reduces passive smoking, increases cessation, lowers consumption, removes role models from children's view
Price: regular increases in the real (adjusted for inflation) price of tobacco products	Reduces consumption and prevalence; especially effective among adolescents
Public education: adequate funding for general and school education on tobacco	Sophisticated, intensive mass media campaigns increase quitting
Promotion: end to exemptions for sporting events and of "product placement"	Important in re-establishing non-smoking as the norm
Proved treatments: subsidies for cessation clinics and proven drug therapies	Counselling, nicotine replacement therapy, and bupropion at least double the success of attempts to quit; cost should not act as barrier to proved cessation aids
Prosecution: increase and publicise efforts to enforce legislation	Publicity has important "knock-on" effect—for example, in reducing sales to minors
Point of sale: tobacco products made an under the counter item	Closes further channel of promotion of tobacco products
Products and their production: remove the exemption for nicotine in tobacco from medicines, food, or other consumer protection legislation	Comprehensive and unified approach needed for regulation of nicotine (and other components in tobacco and tobacco smoke)
Packaging: move to generic packaging	Reduces appeal of tobacco products as symbols of lifestyle, sophistication, and wealth
Probity in public pronouncements: proscribe and penalise misleading public statements about tobacco and the tobacco industry	Reduces misleading information and confusion about tobacco

Good evidence exists that at least the first six of these initiatives are effective

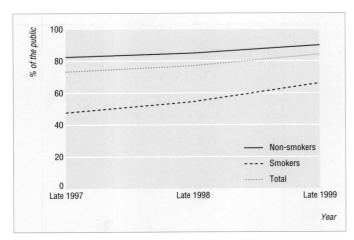

Support for smoke-free restaurants in South Australia (smoke-free policy introduced in January 1999). Adapted from Miller et al (*Aust N Z J Public Health* 2002;26:38-44)

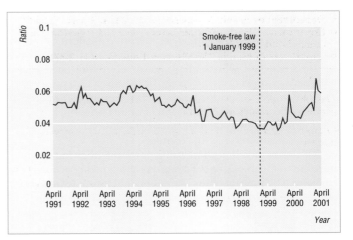

Economics of smoke-free policies in restaurants: ratio of South Australia's restaurant sales to its retail sales, 1991 to 2001. Adapted from Wakefield et al (see Further Reading box)

Price

Price is one of the strongest influences on tobacco consumption. Typically, an increase in price of tobacco products of 10% causes a fall in smoking of 4% in adults and 6% in children, thus reducing prevalence while increasing revenue. Progressive and regular increases in the price of tobacco products through taxation, at least in line with the cost of living and preferably more, can therefore have a considerable impact on smoking prevalence. A price rise should be accompanied by clear publicity about the reasons for it—to reinforce the message that smoking is bad for the pocket as well as for health. A price rise also needs to be associated with appropriate investment to deter and detect smuggling of tobacco products into higher price areas.

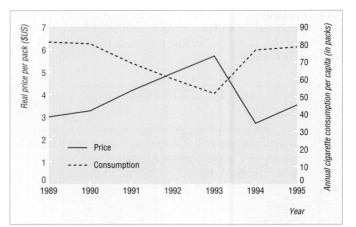

Inverse relation between real price of cigarettes and consumption, Canada, 1989-95. Adapted from Jha et al (*Curbing the epidemic: governments and the economics of tobacco control.* Washington, DC: World Bank, 1999)

Public education

Mass media campaigns have a direct impact on the prevalence of smoking and are most effective when they are sustained and delivered as part of a comprehensive tobacco control programme. Most of the reduction is the result of established smokers quitting, but campaigns also reduce the proportion of children taking up smoking.

Mass media campaigns are expensive but not in relation to levels of tax revenue raised from tobacco products. Effective campaigns need careful coordination and a blend of medical and marketing expertise to ensure that their content is scientifically accurate and their presentation effective.

They also need to be bold and to take some risks, challenging public and personal opinions and feelings so that the issue of tobacco remains "alive" in the minds of individuals and communities. Such activities therefore need to have adequate funds not only for production and dissemination of materials but also for associated programmes of market research.

Strongly enforced non-smoking policies in schools seem to result in a lower prevalence of smoking in schoolchildren, though little evidence exists to date on the longer term effectiveness of this and other school based strategies in preventing smoking.

Evidence is mounting from communities with intensive, population-wide education strategies that the best way of reducing smoking in young people is to reset prevailing norms about smoking and to reduce greatly the prevalence of smoking in adults.

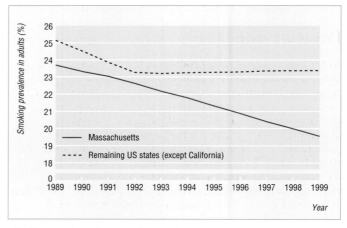

Effectiveness of sustained public education campaigns in reducing smoking in US state of Massachusetts. Adapted from Biener et al (*BMJ* 2000;321:351-4)

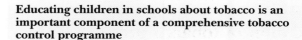

Educating children in schools about tobacco is an important component of a comprehensive tobacco control programme

Promotion

An increasing proportion of governments in Western countries have moved to ban all promotion of cigarettes and smoking via the electronic and print media; outdoor advertising such as billboards; competitions; or via direct "giveaways" to passers by. The Norwegian government was the first to commit itself to such a policy, and the announcement of this decision, in 1970, was followed by an immediate end to the upward trend in tobacco consumption in that country.

This shows the importance of a government giving a clear message to the public that it is serious about taking action on smoking. The passing of the legislation and its implementation are further landmark events that lend themselves to more publicity about changing norms in regard to smoking and the reasons for them.

Banning indirect tobacco advertising through sponsorship in sport and other public areas is as important as ending direct advertising. Other forms of tobacco promotion, such as product

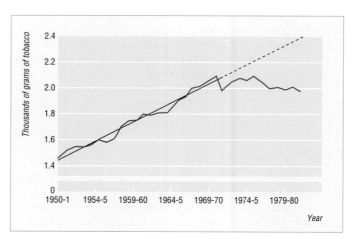

Impact of political commitment to tobacco control—tobacco consumption in Norway before and after the 1975 tobacco act (first discussed 1970), which included a ban on cigarette advertising. Adapted from *Health or Smoking?* (Royal College of Physicians, 1983)

placement (deliberate or otherwise) in films and via the internet, also must be dealt with. This requires coordinated intergovernmental action because these activities transcend national boundaries.

Smoking in films helps to promote a positive image of smoking to young people

Point of sale

As the advertising of their products in the mass media and outdoor venues has come to an end in some countries, tobacco companies have increased the volume and sophistication of their promotional activities indoors in shops selling their products. Anecdotal reports speak of specially designed dispensing racks that obscure health warnings on cigarette packets, and some companies will refit entire display areas of shops in return for a guaranteed share of the space to show off their products. In Western Australia the introduction of a requirement that 50% of the area of promotional posters shown at the point of sale should contain a health warning was followed by a sharp reduction in the use of such posters. An unambiguous law that requires tobacco products to be stored out of sight under the counter (so that customers have to ask for them by name) is much better than governments having to make piecemeal regulatory responses to the industry's attempts to circumvent advertising restrictions.

Regulation of tobacco products

Cigarettes are highly toxic, but in most countries they have generally remained exempt from the food, drug, or consumer protection legislation that applies to other consumer products. Smokeless tobacco products (see chapter 11) are much safer than cigarettes but are not permitted in many countries on health grounds. Medicinal nicotine is even safer, but is generally subject to drug legislation that prevents or inhibits use as an alternative regular nicotine supply. The result is that regulatory systems tend to favour the most dangerous products, and, if so, need to be reformed.

Packaging

As one Australian tobacco company's annual report said, "Our products are their own best advertisement." This statement shows the importance to manufacturers of establishing and maintaining a physical image for each brand, preferably one that makes it symbolic of a desirable lifestyle, sophistication, and wealth. This has led to serious discussion of a move to generic packaging—with tobacco products all being presented in deliberately unappealing packets, with a substantial proportion

---

Prosecution

- Regulatory measures to control tobacco need to be seen to be enforced
- Successful prosecutions of tobacco and advertising companies are an embarrassment to industries whose public images are critical to their business
- Prosecutions and large fines for small players in the industry—such as shopkeepers who repeatedly break the law on selling cigarettes to children or sellers of cut price smuggled tobacco—are also important in signalling that communities and their governments are serious about tobacco control
- Publicising such cases spreads and strengthens that perception and has been effective in persuading proprietors of tobacco outlets to take greater care in instructing their staff not to sell cigarettes to under-age customers

---

The Irish government has recently started to look at the issue of legislation surrounding medicinal nicotine as an alternative regular supply. It has established and is funding an Office for Tobacco Control with a remit to advise the government on tobacco related issues

---

Further reading

- Fichtenberg CM, Glantz SA. Effect of smoke-free workplaces on smoking behaviour: systematic review. *BMJ* 2002;325:188-91.
- Wakefield M, Siahpush M, Scollo M, Lal A, Hyland A, McCaul K, et al. The effect of a smoke-free law on restaurant business in South Australia. *Aust N Z J Public Health* 2002;26:375-82.
- Glantz SA, Slade L, Bero LA, Hanauer P, Barnes DE. *The cigarette papers.* Berkeley: University of California Press, 1996.
- Royal College of Physicians. *Nicotine addiction in Britain: a report of the Tobacco Advisory Group of the Royal College of Physicians.* London: RCP, 2001.

of each packet displaying strong written and visual warnings about the hazards of smoking.

Probity in public pronouncements

The tobacco companies have an increasingly long record of being successfully prosecuted for misleading and deceptive behaviour under trade practices and consumer protection legislation. The Australian state of Tasmania has recognised that dealing with an entrenched pattern of such behaviour by case law and usually civil prosecution is an unsatisfactory way of curbing it. Instead, it has proscribed—and provided penalties for—issuing misleading public statements about either tobacco or the tobacco industry.

The film shot (from *Die Another Day*) is from the Kobal Collection.

Competing interests: KJ received costs for travel and accommodation from SmithKlineBeecham to attend a meeting of the Australian Smoking Cessation Consortium that was convened by the drug company. See chapter 1 for the series editor's competing interests.

Key points

- Effective tobacco control programmes should tackle smoking at the population level
- Health staff working in smoking cessation should know about the main population strategies
- All tobacco advertising, sponsorship, and product placement should be banned
- Smoke-free policies should operate in all public places and workplaces
- Governments should introduce progressive price increases through tax
- Mass media public education programmes are an important strategy
- Effective policing of tobacco laws and smuggling is needed
- Appropriate cessation services should be available to all smokers wanting to quit
- Current inconsistent legislation on tobacco products and medicinal nicotine needs to be reformed

11   Harm reduction

Ann McNeill

Although the ideal for all smokers is to quit completely, a substantial proportion of smokers either do not want to stop smoking or have been unable to do so despite many attempts. Harm reduction strategies are aimed at reducing the adverse health effects of tobacco use in these individuals.

Cutting down

Cutting down on the number of cigarettes smoked each day is a common strategy used by smokers to reduce harm, to move towards quitting, or to save money. Some health professionals also advocate cutting down if smokers cannot or will not stop. No evidence exists, however, that major health risks are reduced by this strategy. The likely explanation for this is that smoking is primarily a nicotine seeking behaviour, and smokers who cut down tend to compensate by taking more and deeper puffs from each cigarette, and smoking more of it. This results in a much smaller proportional reduction in intake of nicotine (and in associated tar and other toxins) than the reduction in number of cigarettes smoked suggests resulting in little net health benefit.

Cutting down on cigarettes in conjunction with the use of nicotine replacement therapy (NRT) to maintain nicotine levels is a more promising strategy, although NRT is not currently licensed in the United Kingdom or in many other countries for use in this way. Preliminary studies have suggested that this approach may help with sustained cigarette reduction and reduce intake of toxins, but no strong evidence exists yet of health benefit from this strategy.

Switching to "low tar" cigarettes

Many smokers who are concerned about the health effects of smoking switch to "low tar" cigarettes, in the belief that these are less dangerous than ordinary cigarettes. This perception has been encouraged by the tobacco industry and, in many countries, also by government policies seeking a progressive reduction in the tar yields of cigarettes.

However, tar yields from cigarettes are measured by machines that artificially "smoke" the cigarettes, and much of the reduction in the tar yield of low tar cigarettes, as measured by a smoking machine, results from ventilation holes introduced in the filter to dilute the smoke drawn in by the machine. The ratio of tar to nicotine produced in the tobacco smoke of low tar cigarettes is in fact closely similar to that of conventional cigarettes. Low tar therefore also means low nicotine.

"Low tar" cigarettes showing ventilation holes in the filters

Prospective hazard ratios for death for smokers who cut down or quit compared with continuing heavy smokers

Cause of death	No of deaths	Adjusted hazard ratio*	95% confidence interval
All causes			
Cutting down	434	1.02	0.89 to 1.17
Quitting	577	0.65	0.56 to 0.74
Cardiovascular diseases†			
Cutting down	138	1.01	0.76 to 1.35
Quitting	171	0.88	0.68 to 1.15
Tobacco related cancer			
Cutting down	70	0.91	0.63 to 1.31
Quitting	51	0.36	0.22 to 0.59
Respiratory disease			
Cutting down	28	1.20	0.70 to 2.07
Quitting	23	0.77	0.44 to 1.35

*Results were obtained from a stratified Cox proportional hazards regression model, with data adjusted for age (underlying), sex, cohort of origin, body mass index, educational level, duration of smoking, and inhalation habits
†These analyses included adjustment for systolic blood pressure (per 10 mmHg increase)
Adapted from Godtfredsen et al

Enabling smokers to take control of their cigarette consumption—by using NRT at the same time as cutting down on smoking—may also increase smokers' confidence and ability to quit subsequently

Equating low tar with "healthy": market research for Silk Cut (manufactured by Gallaher)

"Who are we talking to? The core low tar (and Silk Cut) smoker is female . . . upmarket, aged 25 plus, a smart health conscious professional who feels guilty about smoking but either doesn't want to give it up or can't. Although racked with guilt they feel reassured that in smoking low tar they are making a smart choice and will jump at any chance to make themselves feel better about their habit"
". . . white signals the low tar category . . . low tar ('healthy') quality"

Source: House of Commons Health Committee. *The tobacco industry and the health risks of smoking.* London: Stationery Office, 2000; para 87 (session 1991-200). www.parliament.uk/commons/selcom/hlthhome.htm

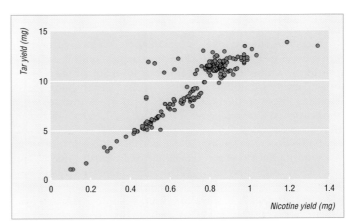

Tar and nicotine yields for 187 cigarette brands tested by UK Laboratory of the Government Chemist (data from www.open.gov.uk/doh/dhhome.htm)

As with cutting down, smokers who switch to lower yield brands tend to compensate for the reduction in nicotine delivery by changing their smoking pattern. With low tar cigarettes smokers do this in two main ways—they smoke the cigarettes more "strongly" by taking more or deeper puffs or they occlude the filter ventilation holes with fingers or lips to prevent or reduce smoke dilution. This results in very little, if any, change in actual intake of nicotine—and consequently of tar—and ultimately therefore, in little reduction in harm.

Switching to cigars or pipes

Some cigarette smokers, particularly men, switch to smoking cigars or pipes as a means of giving up cigarettes. The risks of smoking cigars or pipes for smokers who have never been regular cigarette smokers are indeed much lower than in former cigarette smokers, principally because they tend not to inhale the smoke but rely on nicotine absorption from the buccal mucosa. Cigarette smokers who switch to cigars or pipes tend, however, to continue to inhale the smoke and are therefore likely to gain little or no health benefit.

Alternative cigarettes

Several tobacco companies have designed and in some cases marketed alternative smoking products that heat rather than burn tobacco or tobacco products. An example is the Eclipse brand of cigarettes, now marketed in the United States with the claim of being a safer alternative to conventional cigarettes. Eclipse delivers less tar than conventional cigarettes, but more carbon monoxide, so any harm reduction is likely to be limited. No studies have yet shown health benefits associated with switching to Eclipse or similar alternative smoking products.

Switching to smokeless tobacco

Smokeless tobacco comes in two main forms—snuff and chewing tobacco. The types of smokeless tobacco product used around the world vary considerably, as do the health risks across the products used. For example, in India, use of smokeless tobacco is a major cause of oral cancer. Nevertheless the health risks associated with smokeless tobacco are considerably smaller than those associated with cigarettes.

In Sweden the use of oral moist snuff (known as snus) has been common among men for several decades. The health risks of this product seem to be extremely low, in absolute terms as well as in relation to cigarette smoking. Snus seems to be widely used by smokers as an alternative to cigarettes, contributing to the low overall prevalence of smoking and smoking related disease in Sweden.

Snus and other smokeless oral tobacco products currently being developed by some tobacco companies could therefore provide a viable alternative to smoking for many smokers in other countries, and thus deliver substantial health gains. However, these products are currently prohibited throughout the European Union (except in Sweden) on the grounds that they are unsafe.

Some experts have argued that even if smokeless tobacco is a less harmful form of nicotine intake than smoking, its availability might have unintended undesirable consequences, such as causing harm to people who might have otherwise quit smoking completely or attracting young people to tobacco use. Other experts recommend that smokers should be able to choose less harmful forms of nicotine delivery. They argue that the ban on the less harmful smokeless tobacco products

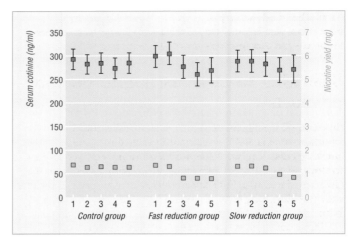

Effect of compensation by smokers when smoking low tar cigarettes, as shown by mean blood levels of cotinine (with 95% confidence intervals) and related nicotine yield over time. 1=run-in to study; 2=entry; 3=at 2 months; 4=at 4 months; 5=at 6 months. Adapted from Frost et al (*Thorax* 1995;50:1038-43)

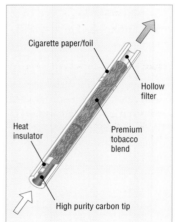

According to the manufacturer, R J Reynolds (RJR), Eclipse cigarettes are "designed to burn only about 3% as much tobacco as other cigarettes." RJR also explains that they "create smoke primarily by heating tobacco rather than burning it" (www.eclipse.rjrt.com)

Swedish snus, with pound coins for scale

Some experts say that if smokers switched to the least harmful forms of smokeless tobacco it would substantially reduce their harm

should be lifted—within an evidence based regulatory framework that favours the least harmful forms of smokeless tobacco—and that smokers should be encouraged to use them.

Switching to pharmaceutical nicotine products

Switching from cigarettes to pharmaceutical nicotine products—that is, NRT—is standard practice in managing smoking cessation, but these products are not currently licensed for long term use as an alternative to smoking. Given that the risks associated with NRT are much lower than those associated with smoking, long term use of NRT products is a rational harm reduction strategy.

However, as most smokers do not find the current NRT products to be as satisfying as cigarettes, the viability of these products as a long term substitute is limited. The technology to develop safe, inhaled forms of nicotine that could provide a more satisfactory alternative to cigarette smoking is available in the pharmaceutical industry, but in the context of the current regulatory framework in the United Kingdom and many other countries, such products would not be licensed and are therefore not commercially viable. As discussed above and in the previous article in this series, this imbalance in the regulation of nicotine needs to be redressed urgently in favour of public health.

The table showing prospective hazard ratios for death for smokers who cut down or quit is adapted from Godfredsen et al (*Am J Epidemiol* 2002;156:994-1001).

Competing interests: Ann McNeill has received two honorariums and hospitality from manufacturers of tobacco dependence treatments. See chapter 1 for the series editor's competing interests.

Key points

- Many smokers try to reduce the harm from smoking by cutting down or switching to "low tar" products
- No evidence exists that cutting down or switching to low tar products substantially reduces health risks
- Cutting down on cigarettes with concomitant use of NRT could be a more promising strategy
- Switching to smokeless tobacco should substantially reduce adverse effects from tobacco use, but in many countries its use is illegal
- Switching to pharmaceutical nicotine would substantially reduce harm, but NRT products are licensed as cessation aids, not as substitutes, and smokers tend to find them less satisfying than cigarettes
- The regulatory framework in many countries, including Britain, discourages the development of nicotine products that are less harmful than cigarettes

Further reading

- Tobacco Advisory Group of the Royal College of Physicians. Regulation of nicotine intake by smokers, and implications for health. In: *Nicotine addiction in Britain.* London: RCP, 2000. (A report of the Tobacco Advisory Group of the Royal College of Physicians, Chapter 6.)
- Stratton K, Shetty P, Wallace R, Bondurant S, eds. *Clearing the smoke: assessing the science base for tobacco harm reduction.* Washington, DC: National Academy Press, 2001.
- Ferrence R, Slade J, Room R, Pope M, eds. *Nicotine and public health.* Washington, DC: American Public Health Association, 2000.
- Tobacco Advisory Group of the Royal College of Physicians. *Protecting smokers, saving lives. The case for a tobacco and nicotine regulation authority.* London: RCP, 2002.
- National Cancer Institute. *Risks associated with smoking cigarettes and low machine-measured yields of tar and nicotine.* Bethesda, MD: US Department of Health and Human Services, National Institutes of Health, National Cancer Institute, 2001. (Smoking and tobacco control monograph No 13; NIH publication No 02-5074.)

12 Economics of smoking cessation

Steve Parrott, Christine Godfrey

Smoking imposes a huge economic burden on society—currently up to 15% of total healthcare costs in developed countries. Smoking cessation can save years of life, at a very low cost compared with alternative interventions. This chapter reviews some of the economic aspects of smoking cessation.

Who benefits from cessation?

The most obvious benefits of smoking cessation are improvements in life expectancy and prevention of disease. However, cessation also improves individuals' quality of life as smokers tend to have a lower self reported health status than non-smokers, and this improves after stopping smoking.

There are also wider economic benefits to individuals and society, arising from reductions in the effects of passive smoking in non-smokers and savings to the health service and the employer. These wider benefits are often omitted from economic evaluations of cessation interventions, which consequently tend to underestimate the true value for money afforded by such programmes.

Economic burden of smoking

Many estimates have been made of the economic cost of smoking in terms of health resources. For the United States they typically range from about 0.6% to 0.85% of gross domestic product. In absolute terms, the US public health service estimates a total cost of $50bn (£29bn; €42bn) a year for the treatment of smoking related diseases, in addition to an annual $47bn in lost earnings and productivity. Estimated total costs in Australia and Canada, as a proportion of their gross domestic product, are 0.4% and 0.56% respectively. In the United Kingdom, the treatment of smoking related disease has been estimated to cost the NHS £1.4bn-£1.5bn a year (about 0.16% of the gross domestic product)—including £127m to treat lung cancer alone.

When expressed as a percentage of gross domestic product, the economic burden of smoking seems to be rising. In reality, however, the burden may not be increasing, but instead, as more diseases are known to be attributable to smoking, the burden attributed to smoking increases. Earlier estimates may simply have underestimated the true cost.

Passive smoking

In the United States, passive smoking has been estimated to be responsible for 19% of total expenditure on childhood respiratory conditions, and maternal smoking has been shown to increase healthcare expenditure by $120 a year for children under age 5 years and $175 for children under age 2 years.

In the United Kingdom an estimated £410m a year is spent treating childhood illness related to passive smoking; in adults, passive smoking accounts for at least 1000 deaths in non-smokers, at an estimated cost of about £12.8m a year at 2002 prices.

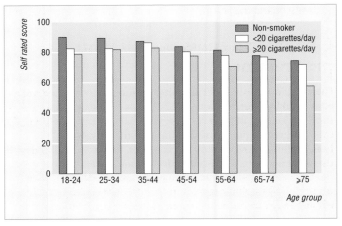

Self rated health status (100 = best imaginable health state), by age and smoking status. Data from Kind et al. *UK population norms for EQ-5D*. York: Centre for Health Economics (Discussion paper 172)

Benefits of smoking cessation

Smokers and their families
- Improved quality and quantity of life for those stopping smoking
- Improved quality and quantity of life for those living with smokers through a reduction in the harm from passive smoking

Society
- Lower healthcare expenditure on treatment of smoking induced disease
- Less workplace absenteeism due to smoking related disease
- Less harm from passive smoking in public places
- Reduction in costs related to cleaning up after smokers (cigarette ends, ash, etc and damage from these to floors and furnishings)

In Puerto Rico, China (above), and Venezuela, the cost of smoking has been estimated as 0.3%-0.43% of the gross domestic product

Passive smoking causes illness and premature loss of life, at all ages from the prenatal period to late adult life

Cost of absenteeism

Absenteeism arising from smoking related disease is also a major cause of lost productivity, a cost incurred by employers. An annual estimated 34 million days are lost in England and Wales through sickness absence resulting from smoking related illness, and in Scotland the cost of this productivity loss is about £400m.

Cost effectiveness of cessation programmes

Clear evidence exists that smoking cessation interventions are effective. However, to show value for money, the costs as well as the effectiveness of such programmes have to be examined. The overwhelming evidence is that face to face cessation interventions provide excellent value for money compared with the great majority of other medical interventions.

Several complex factors influence cost effectiveness. For example, although a cessation programme tends to be more effective as its intensity increases, increased intensity is associated with increased costs, therefore increasing both sides of the cost effectiveness ratio. This was illustrated in a study by Parrott et al (1998) of the range of intensities of smoking cessation interventions in the United Kingdom. The researchers examined these interventions using local cost data and life years saved as predicted from the PREVENT simulation model. They looked at four interventions: a basic intervention of three minutes of opportunistic brief advice; brief advice plus self help material; brief advice plus self help material and nicotine replacement products; and brief advice plus self help material, nicotine replacement products, and a recommendation to attend a smoking cessation clinic. The most cost effective intervention was the brief advice alone (cost £159 per life year saved, £248 when discounted at 6%), although the most intensive clinical interventions still represent good value for money at £1002 per life year saved when discounted at 6%.

The cost effectiveness of putting the US Agency for Healthcare Research and Quality's clinical guidelines on smoking cessation into practice has also been estimated, for combined interventions based on smokers' preferences for different types of the five basic recommended interventions. The cost of implementation was estimated at $6.3bn in the first year, as a result of which society would gain 1.7 million new quitters at an average cost of $3779 per quitter, $2587 per life year saved, and $1915 per quality adjusted life year (QALY). In this study the most intensive interventions were calculated to be more cost effective than the briefer therapies.

Care should be taken when extrapolating the results of these evaluations, as cost effectiveness estimates are likely to be time and country specific and highly dependent on the healthcare system in question. In a system of fee for service, as in the United States, monetary rewards may be necessary to encourage provision. On the other hand, if patients who stop smoking place a reduced burden on the primary care budget in future years, the incentives to provide such services may be inherent in the system.

Pharmacological interventions

The National Institute for Clinical Excellence (NICE) has recently estimated the cost effectiveness of using nicotine replacement therapy (NRT) or bupropion therapy. These estimates projected life years saved over a shorter period than the PREVENT model and hence produced generally higher figures: £1000-£2400 per life year saved for advice and NRT,

---

Smoking related fires cause about £151m of damage each year in England and Wales

---

Cost effectiveness estimates for healthcare providers

Type of intervention	Costs per life year saved (£)	
	Undiscounted	Discounted
Face to face		
Brief advice	159	248
Brief advice plus self help	195	303
Brief advice plus self help plus NRT	524	815
Brief advice plus self help plus NRT plus specialist cessation service	658	1022
Community		
"Quit and win" programme:		
Medium intensity	634	986
"No smoking" day	26	40
Broader community health promotion interventions (medium intensity)	192	295

NRT = nicotine replacement therapy. Data from Parrott et al, 1998 (see Further Reading box), revised to reflect 2001-2 prices.

Discounting is a method of adjusting for the fact that individuals prefer to incur costs in later periods and enjoy benefits in the current period. Applying a discount rate transforms future values into current values, taking this preference into account

---

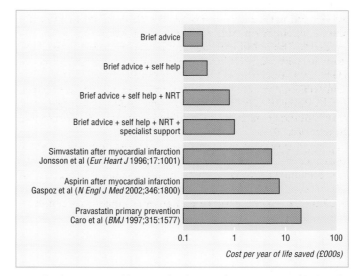

Cost effectiveness of smoking cessation interventions compared with that of routine strategies for preventing myocardial infarction

---

The National Institute for Clinical Excellence is part of the NHS in England and Wales; it issues guidance on current "best practice"

£645-£1500 for advice plus bupropion, and £890-£1970 for advice, nicotine replacement, and bupropion. When QALYs are used, the ranges are £741-£1780, £473-£1100, and £660-£1460 respectively. These costs again compare favourably with a range of other healthcare interventions. Bupropion does seem more cost effective than NRT, although the evidence base for the effectiveness of bupropion is much less extensive than for NRT, and results should therefore be treated with caution.

The cost effectiveness of bupropion has been investigated in Spain with a decision model (Musin et al, eighth meeting of the Society for Research on Nicotine and Tobacco, Savannah, 2002). The model presents results in an incremental analysis over and above opportunistic advice in primary care. The findings show that if all motivated smokers in Spain were to use the therapy, over a 20 year period 44 235 smoking related deaths would be averted at a saving to the healthcare system of €1.25bn. In the United States, studies have predicted savings of between $8.8m and $14m over 20 years when bupropion is added to an insurance plan. In a UK study, Stapleton et al (1999) used data from a randomised placebo controlled trial of nicotine patches and a survey of resource use to show that if general practitioners were allowed to prescribe transdermal nicotine patches on the NHS for 12 weeks, the cost per life year saved would be £398 for people aged under 35, £345 for those aged 35-44, £432 for those aged 45-54, and £785 for those aged 55-65. Since Stapleton's study was published, NRT has been made available in Britain through NHS prescription. However, studies have tended to exclude potential side effects of bupropion and are again based on a more limited effectiveness database then the evidence for the effectiveness of NRT products.

The means by which the provision is financed is a crucial determinant of the effectiveness of smoking cessation products. Evidence shows that smokers are more likely to take up smoking cessation interventions if they are provided by their insurance scheme or health service than if they have to pay for them themselves. In the United Kingdom, NHS provision can reduce costs through bulk buying and discounts from pharmaceutical manufacturers. The price for a packet of seven 15 mg Nicorette patches, for example, costs £15.99 through retail outlets, compared with an NHS purchase price of only £9.07, a reduction of about 43%. It is also clear that decreases in the price of NRT products and increases in the price of cigarettes would lead to substantial increases in per capita sales of NRT products.

The photograph of the Marlboro advertisement in China is published with permission from Mark Henley/Panos.

Competing interests: See chapter 1 for the series editor's competing interests.

Comparative costs of other common healthcare treatments (analysis of guidance of the National Institute for Clinical Excellence)

Intervention	Incremental cost (£)	
	Per quality adjusted life year	Per life year gained
Zanamivir in managing influenza	9300-31 500	
Taxanes for ovarian cancer		6500-10 000
Taxanes for breast cancer		7000-24 000
Implantable cardioverter defibrillators for arrhythmias		26 000-31 000
Glycoprotein IIb/IIIa inhibitors for acute coronary syndromes		7000-12 000
Methylphenidate for attention-deficit/hyperactivity disorder in children	10 000-15 000	
Tribavirin and interferon alfa for hepatitis C:		
First six months' treatment	3000-7000	
Second six months' treatment	5000-36 000	
Laparoscopic surgery for inguinal hernias	50 000	
Riluzole for motor neurone disease	34 000-43 000	
Orlistat for obesity in adults		20 000-30 000

Adapted from Raftery (*BMJ* 2001;323:1300-3).

Key points

- Savings to the healthcare system, a reduction in the harm caused by passive smoking, and savings to employers are all relevant in evaluations of cessation interventions
- The economic cost of smoking in the United States may be as high as 1.15% of gross domestic product in terms of healthcare costs alone
- The estimated cost to the NHS is £1.4bn-£1.5bn
- Cessation interventions offer excellent value for money when compared with some other healthcare interventions
- Some studies have quantified outcomes in life years saved, not allowing for changes in quality of life, thereby underestimating the cost effectiveness of smoking cessation by almost half

Further reading

- Action on Smoking and Heath. *Smoking and disease. Basic facts No 2.* London: ASH, 2002. www.ash.org.uk (accessed 15 Dec 2003).
- Cromwell J, Bartosch WJ, Fiore MC, Hasselblad V, Baker T. Cost-effectiveness of the clinical practice recommendations in the AHCPR guideline for smoking cessation. *JAMA* 1997;278:1759-66.
- Nielsen K, Fiore MC. Cost-benefit analysis of sustained-release bupropion, nicotine patch, or both for smoking cessation. *Prev Med* 2000;30:209-16.
- Parrott S, Godfrey C, Raw M, West R, McNeill, A. Guidance for commissioners on the cost effectiveness of smoking cessation interventions. *Thorax* 1998;53(suppl 5, part 2):S1-38.
- Stapleton JA, Lowin A, Russell MAH. Prescription of transdermal nicotine patches for smoking cessation in general practice: evaluation of cost-effectiveness. *Lancet* 1999;354:210-5.

13 Policy priorities for tobacco control

Konrad Jamrozik

Although many countries have implemented strategies for reducing tobacco use at individual and population level, no country to date has adopted a truly comprehensive control programme. In addition, the tobacco industry and the strategies it uses to counteract policies on tobacco control and thereby maintain and develop its commercial markets have both continued to evolve. All communities therefore face at least some "unfinished business" in relation to tobacco control, and those working in smoking cessation need to be familiar with the necessary policy responses.

The healthcare industry

Individuals and institutions in the healthcare industry have an important exemplar role. In many countries the prevalence of smoking among doctors differs little from that in the wider community. This considerably undermines individual practitioners' credibility in advising patients not to smoke and denies the profession as a whole the influence it might wield on public and political opinion and policy on tobacco.

Institutions that train health professionals need to make more time available in both undergraduate and postgraduate curriculums for teaching about smoking and especially about effective cessation interventions. Coverage of these topics is currently, for the most part, inadequate. As assessment shapes learning, these topics also need to feature prominently and regularly in major examinations.

All healthcare facilities, including schools of medicine, nursing, and dentistry, should adopt and enforce comprehensive smoke-free policies across their entire campuses and not just in buildings. Where smoking rooms are provided for inpatients, these should have separate, externally ventilated air conditioning systems so that tobacco smoke is not recirculated into the rest of the building.

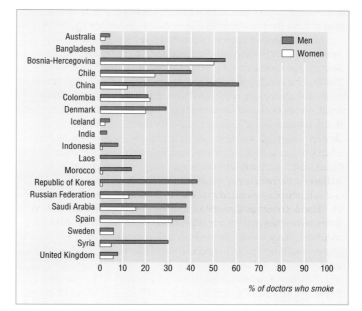

Prevalence of smoking among doctors around the world, according to data collected from 493 medical schools in 93 countries (36% response rate) in 1995. Data from Mackay et al (*The tobacco atlas.* Geneva: World Health Organization, 2002)

> **One of the most simple and cost effective of all medical interventions is for doctors to tell every smoker they encounter in their work that giving up the habit is one of the most important things they can do for their health. Ascertaining smoking status and intervening as appropriate must become a routine component of all health care**

Policies on smoke-free places

The smoking of tobacco should eventually become an activity undertaken only by consenting adults in private. Although such a goal seems unattainable now, many current smoke-free policies were at one time viewed in the same way.

In several countries, virtually all workplaces and public buildings (and other enclosed public places) are now smoke-free zones, with equivalent policies spreading steadily into venues such as outdoor sports arenas, as well as into private homes. An important omission has been schools, where smoke-free policies should cover not only buildings but also playgrounds. They should also extend to all school related events, including parents' meetings, excursions, and field trips. Several countries are seriously considering legislation to ban smoking in private cars carrying infants or children.

Overall, it is now possible to conceive of communities where incremental changes will result in all public places becoming smoke free—and free also of all of the litter generated by smokers.

Examples of stickers available in Australia to show visitors that private homes and cars are smoke-free environments

Advertising and sponsorship

The tobacco industry has proved adept in identifying and exploiting loopholes in legislation designed to restrict how it advertises its products. Recent examples include the industry's expansion of in-store advertising—as advertising outdoors and in the mass media becomes illegal. Ultimately, tobacco products should become "under the counter" items that are not displayed and must be requested by name. Such an arrangement is entirely appropriate to the harm they do and their proper "adults only" status.

Given their danger—half of cigarette smokers who continue to smoke are killed prematurely by the habit—legislation on promotion of tobacco needs to cover all kinds of products and define promotional activities widely. Governments have been slow, for example, to deal with "same name" advertising (that is, advertising of other products carrying the cigarette's brand name, such as Marlboro clothing) and "product placement" (whereby celebrities or producers of entertainment are paid to use and display particular tobacco products prominently).

The internet is already becoming a vehicle for unsolicited direct advertising of tobacco to children as well as to adults, making it even worse than sponsorship of international sport. Solving each of these problems requires a coordinated international response.

Young people and smoking?

Rather than targeting children and teenagers, the best method of helping them not to start smoking is highly likely to be a policy of systematically driving down the prevalence of smoking among adults. Already evidence shows that young people in communities with active and prominent general programmes of tobacco control are beginning to realise that saying "no thanks, I've given up" is more "adult" than accepting the offer of a cigarette.

"Quit" campaigns directed specifically at teenagers have not received much attention to date, despite the fact that in many populations two thirds of those who ever try smoking abandon the habit before their mid-20s.

Nicotine and tobacco regulation

A comprehensive approach to tobacco control must also include systematic attention to the tobacco products themselves and to their presentation to the public. Tobacco companies, including those run as government monopolies, have to be flushed out from behind their "commercial and sensitive" smokescreen and be required to declare fully what they add to their products during manufacture, just as the makers of virtually all other products intended for human consumption are obliged to do.

Many governments have already abandoned voluntary agreements with tobacco companies on health warnings to be displayed on their products because the manufacturers regularly resist using those warnings that independent field testing show to be most arresting.

Governments are under pressure to move on from mandating warnings of proved effectiveness by requiring plain "generic" packaging that is far less eye catching. Such regulation needs to be complemented by "probity" clauses that make it an offence to make misleading or untrue public pronouncements about tobacco products, their effects, and the activities of the tobacco industry in general.

Public and school education

- The international benchmark in this area has been set by the US state of California, where the budget for tobacco control has been about $5 (£2.70; €3.90)—over 1.5 times the average retail price of a packet of 20 cigarettes—per head of population per year
- This kind of investment makes sustained, sophisticated, public and school based education campaigns eminently feasible
- Doctors and other health professionals must press their own governments to match California's commitment

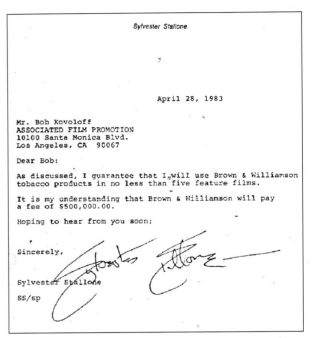

Letter from US actor Sylvester Stallone agreeing in 1983 to smoke Brown & Williamson products in five feature films in exchange for $500 000. From the Legacy Tobacco Documents Library at University of California, San Francisco (http://legacy.library.ucsf.edu)

"Quit" campaigns need to be targeted at teenage smokers, not just older smokers

Price, taxation, and smuggling

- Studies have clearly shown that all smokers—and particularly young smokers—are sensitive to the price of tobacco products
- Geographic variations in the "real" or absolute prices of tobacco products, however, soon lead to the emergence of considerable smuggling
- Ample evidence shows that organised crime is deeply involved in smuggling, and detailed studies of international movements of tobacco products have led to questions about possible connivance in these activities by major tobacco manufacturers
- Local detection and enforcement activities can never hope to deal adequately with such problems
- Technical solutions such as unambiguous, tamper-proof marking of packets of tobacco products to indicate their origin and tax paid status will form only part of the answer
- Coordinated international action is needed to tackle smuggling

Strong arguments exist for consolidating into a single statutory instrument all legislation covering tobacco and nicotine and for imposing price and marketing restrictions on products in direct and consistent relation to their potential risk

The tobacco industry

The tobacco industry operates as a global entity while simultaneously maintaining notable sensitivity and responsiveness to local regulatory and other conditions. Its standard tactics are to debate almost endlessly the scientific evidence on the harm caused by its products, to cultivate (and regularly pay) spokespeople in other industries and in academia, and to purchase influence by making substantial donations to any political party that will accept them. Many of these strategies are designed to foster uncertainty in the minds of the public and governments, and all serve ultimately to delay effective action on tobacco control.

The industry has responded to the growing number of stronger initiatives by Western governments, however, by shifting its primary focus to developing countries. Several factors in these countries conspire to cause needless repetition in this century of the sad experience of tobacco use in the Western world in the last: a lack of information; the long lead time between an increase in the prevalence of smoking and the consequent increase in the incidence of death and disease; and the appeal to farmers of a cash crop and to governments of considerable taxation revenues. Unless effective action is taken globally, more than a billion people will be killed by tobacco this century.

The Framework Convention on Tobacco Control

Such calculations prompted the World Health Organization to convene, in 1999, the first of a series of meetings to draw up an international treaty on tobacco control—that is, an effective global response to a problem already of global scale.

The Framework Convention on Tobacco Control comprises a core statement complemented by several separate instruments that individual governments may or may not adopt. Progress on drafting the document was slowed by considerable resistance from governments of countries that are home to major tobacco companies or that run state tobacco monopolies. The core document was adopted unanimously, however, by the 192 member countries of the World Health Assembly on 21 May 2003, just six days short of the 53rd anniversary of the publication of the first case-control study on smoking and lung cancer. Health professionals everywhere must now press their own governments to ensure that the convention is ratified and enacted in their own countries with minimum delay.

The campaign stickers are from ACOSH (Australia Council on Smoking and Health, www.acosh.org/); the letter from Sylvester Stallone is from the Legacy Tobacco Documents Library at the University of California at San Francisco (http://legacy.library.ucsf.edu); and the photograph above is published with permission from Chris Stowers/Panos.

Despite the strategies and tactics of the tobacco industry, smoking is firmly on the wane in most of the developed world, with the scope and momentum of governmental initiatives growing steadily

The tobacco industry is now targeting its products increasingly at developing countries

Key points
- No country has adopted a truly comprehensive programme on tobacco control, so all nations have some "unfinished business"
- Health professionals should set an example by not smoking
- All public places and workplaces should become smoke free
- Adequate funding and political support should be available for sustained and sophisticated public education campaigns
- Traditional and emerging forms of tobacco advertising should be eliminated
- Effective action is needed on tobacco smuggling
- Legislation on production, packaging, sale, and use of tobacco products should be integrated
- International action—via the Framework Convention on Tobacco Control—is vital in countering the tobacco industry's activities

Further reading
- Richmond R, ed. *Educating medical students about tobacco: planning and implementation*. Paris: International Union Against Tobacco and Lung Disease, 1996.
- Jha P, Chaloupka FJ. *Curbing the epidemic: governments and the economics of tobacco control*. Washington, DC: World Bank, 1999.
- Glantz SA, Slade L, Bero LA, Hanauer P, Barnes DE. *The cigarette papers*. Berkeley: University of California Press, 1996.

Competing interests: KJ received costs for travel and accommodation from SmithKlineBeecham to attend a meeting of the Australian Smoking Cessation Consortium that was convened by the drug company. See chapter 1 for the series editor's competing interests.

Index

As smoking cessation is the subject of this book, all index entries refer to this unless otherwise indicated. Page references in *italics* refer to tables or boxed material; page numbers in **bold** refer to figures.